STRAIGHT TALK

Answers from God's Word

✳✳

MARK JESKE

CONCORDIA  AINT LOUIS

Published by Concordia Publishing House
3558 S. Jefferson Avenue, St. Louis, MO 63118-3968
1-800-325-3040 • www.cph.org

Manufactured in the United States of America

1 2 3 4 5 6 7 8 9 10   21 20 19 18 17 16 15 14 13 12

Table of Contents

DEDICATION

I'd like to dedicate this little book to my friend and partner Jim Johnson, who has served as *Time of Grace*'s president almost from the beginning. His passion and commitment to Gospel outreach through mass media never droop, and his love for people and attention and care to make every interaction with *Time of Grace* a happy one make it a joy for all who work here.

INTRODUCTION

They say that curiosity killed the cat.

That may be good advice when it comes to kids experimenting with household electricity, but it is terrible advice when it comes to the Bible. God's Word is a gold mine of wisdom and knowledge about the construction of the physical universe, the mysteries of human behavior, and the thought processes of God Himself.

However, that wonderful book can often seem daunting—1,500 pages of narrative that took place over two millennia ago. I love it when our *Time of Grace* viewers and readers are curious about what God is up to and send me their questions. This book, *Straight Talk,* is a collection of more than one hundred of those questions, which will certainly include some of your own. Here also are my answers to those questions, which I hope will let God's voice bring information, love, and guidance from His wonderful Word.

I hope that you enjoy the Q & A, and I also hope that you enjoy watching *Time of Grace*'s broadcasts, reading our publications, and downloading information from our **www.timeofgrace.org** Web site.

Pastor Mark Jeske

1

"Your word is a lamp to my feet and a light to my path." (Psalm 119:105)

THE BIBLE

Q: Who wrote the Bible?

A: There are three answers to this seemingly simple question. The first and most important answer is that all its content was motivated, provided, and controlled by God the Holy Spirit Himself. **"All Scripture is breathed out by God,"** says 2 Timothy 3:16. **"Men spoke from God as they were carried along by the Holy Spirit"** (2 Peter 1:21). This is what gives the Bible its power, authority, truth, clarity, consistency, and essential unity, even though the book was assembled over the course of 1,600 years, from the time of Moses to that of the apostle John.

A second answer is that God used human writers as His channels, and He used their vocabularies, ministries, and experiences to give unique purpose and flavor to each of the Bible's sixty-six books. Many authors are known by name; others, such as the writer of Hebrews, are not known. There are also many literary styles and formats in the Holy Book: history, law, poetry and songs, dialogue, sermons, letters, and prophecy.

A third answer is that some of the original manuscripts were written down by an amanuensis, which is a fancy word for personal secretary. Tertius, for instance, did the physical work of putting ink to papyrus in the writing of Romans, as dictated to him by Paul (Romans 16:22).

All that said, even with many writers and scribes, written over many centuries and in three different languages (Hebrew, Aramaic, and Greek), the Bible has one source and one overriding purpose: **"These are written so that you may believe that Jesus is the Christ, the Son of God, and that by believing you may have life in His name"** (John 20:31).

Q: My sister-in-law acquainted me with your messages a year ago, and I have been blessed by them. However, your broadcast message today troubled me. You spoke about four different ways God spoke to people in the past (i.e., direct revelation by *God Himself* to individuals, revelation through prophets and apostles who *spoke* God's words, the personal appearance on earth of *Jesus Christ* as the Word made flesh, and revelation through the *written* Word). I feel you have rejected the fact that God speaks directly to us today. He speaks to our spirit through His Holy Spirit. God truly does speak to us if we let Him.

A: This is an important question and one that has very different answers in the religious world today. On the one hand, has God spoken directly to individuals in the past? Absolutely. Yes, He has. Second, could God do that today if He wanted? Of course. But is that a promise that God has actually made to every believer today? I don't see that anywhere in the Bible.

God has indeed chosen and designated certain people to be apostles and prophets, just as He has chosen to give apostles and prophets some certain supernatural powers to verify that they are God's personal spokespeople. Elijah, Elisha, Paul, and Peter were actually given the ability to raise people from the dead, for example, to authenticate their prophetic or apostolic mission.

However, that doesn't mean that every believer has been given that ability. The only way you and I will know for sure what God has said is through His Scriptures, **"which are able to make you wise for salvation through faith in Christ Jesus"** (2 Timothy 3:15). I have had troubling experiences with people who have said to me, "Pastor Mark, God told me this" or "God told me that," and their information has turned out not to be true.

One dear woman in our community told me that God had spoken to her personally and promised her that she was going to be able to open up a health food restaurant on King Drive just a few blocks away. That was twenty years ago, and there still is no health food restaurant there and she has since moved out of the neighborhood. That "personal revelation from God" was her own dream and desire, which she attributed (wrongly) to God.

Another woman, who was in a troubled marriage, told me, "I feel that God would want me to divorce my husband." In fact, if you look in the Bible, God says all marriages belong to Him and **"what therefore God has joined together, let not men separate"** (Matthew 19:6). God's opinion of marital breakup? Malachi 2:16 brings the real voice of God: **"I hate divorce"** (NIV). Her own wishes to ditch this man were so strong that she supposed that the urges and impulses she felt were really coming from God.

You know, Satan has access to our minds, and he brings all kinds of temptations. He hates the Bible and would like you to think you don't need it. For a sad example of how a lying spirit can infiltrate someone claiming to be a prophet, read 2 Chronicles 18.

Experiences like these cause me to be suspicious of anybody who claims to have the prophetic or apostolic gift of direct personal revelation. Do you want to know how God thinks and what He wants? Go to the Bible. Everything you need to know for your life and for your eternity is found there: Scripture is able indeed to make you wise for salvation through faith in Christ Jesus.

Q: What does the Bible say about creation versus evolution?

A: Charles Darwin, author of *The Origin of Species,* may have done more damage to Christianity than any other human being. His theories of natural selection and survival of the fittest have achieved widespread acceptance in academic and scientific circles. Even many Christians today believe that evolution is a better answer than creation to explain the existence of the physical universe and the people and animals that live in it.

Evolution is based on several bedrock principles:

- There is no intelligent design in nature—plants, animals, people, or earth. Every complex organism got that way spontaneously.

- There was never any massive intervention in the physical universe by an all-powerful God. The universe is a closed system.

- A gigantic explosion (the "Big Bang") left among its debris eight planets in permanent orbit around a flaming gas ball. Not planned. Total coincidence that rock number three had an atmosphere and could sustain organic life.

- At first, earth had only inorganic matter. The inorganic matter spontaneously became organic; organic matter became amoebas, which spontaneously developed into aquatic creatures that developed into humans.

- All these upwardly evolutionary changes in life-forms took many billions of years to occur.

- Since there is no Creator, people are not accountable to any higher authority.

- There is no design or meaning to human existence; we are on our own to come up with some kind of meaning.

There is no possible way to reconcile creation and evolution; those who try end up with neither. The Bible (read Genesis 1–2) has a vastly different account for the origin of the physical universe and its myriad life-forms:

- A supreme, omnipotent, all-knowing God planned and carried out the creation of a fully formed, functioning, mature-appearing universe in six twenty-four-hour days.

- God created the universe with the appearance of age—the first people came into existence as adults, not babies; trees had rings and fruit on their first day, and so on.

- People were designed and created in their present form; they did not evolve from "lower" animals, such as chimpanzees.

- Every person on earth is accountable to the Maker of it.

- The world was made as a beautiful home for God's human creatures; they were appointed to care for it and enjoy it; the purpose for human life is to enjoy a happy relationship with God and to serve Him and one another.

Q: How do I prove to my unbelieving co-worker that God really exists?

A: You will probably never be able to "prove" anything to your friend's satisfaction. But there are three powerful witnesses to

God's existence that He has provided for us—if these don't reveal Him to your friend, nothing will.

1. Nature itself. The Bible says that "the heavens declare the glory of God, and the sky above proclaims His handiwork" (Psalm 19:1). Any unbiased look at the physical universe will have to conclude that there is intelligent design behind our world's incredible beauty, complexity, organization, and life-forms.

2. Conscience. All people, even unbelievers, even people who have never heard a word of Scripture, have a built-in system of knowing the rudiments of right and wrong. When people defy God's will and run from Him, they feel guilt. You can deny guilt, drug it, try to distract yourself from it, or rationalize it, but you can't make it go away. Only Jesus Christ can take away human guilt. We will be restless until we rest in Him (St. Augustine said that).

3. The Bible. That wonderful book contains not only the information your friend needs but also the power to convert his or her heart and change his or her life.

Q: I've been asked how I know the Bible is true. Usually, the person asking wants some sort of proof. What do I tell someone who asks?

A: A similar question with a similar answer. No court of law, no scientific study, no government project, and no think tank will ever be able to "prove" the Bible's accuracy.

Becoming a believer is sort of like falling in love. You can't argue someone into loving someone else; reason and logic don't do it. It is authentic contact with the person that does it. In the same way, you won't get very far by arguing with people about the rightness of your views and the wrongness of theirs. Just let them read or hear God's Word. That's where the power is; that's where the truth is; that's where the draw is.

The power to convert someone to God's truth doesn't come from us. In 1 Corinthians 12:3, Paul says, **"No one can say 'Jesus is Lord' except in the Holy Spirit."** The power comes from reading this great love story and realizing that you are the object of the Father's creative love, the Son's redeeming love, and the Spirit's inspiring love.

Q: Why did God create a world that He knew would fall into sin?

A: This question has plagued children for centuries, and grown-ups wonder about it too. There is really only one possible answer. Our heavenly Father's great desire in fashioning the universe and peopling it with human creatures made to be like Him was to enjoy fellowship with *family,* with His *children.* His aching desire was to be loved, trusted, and obeyed. His aching desire was to spoil us rotten with gifts, delights, and experiences of His goodness. His aching desire was that we would then treat one another the way He treats us—with kindness, love, and a servantheart.

However, if obedience is compelled, it is not free and it is not love. Obedience that is performed out of fear of punishment is just coercion. Only if it were freely given could our response to God be called love, and He risked everything to gain our love. We betrayed Him. He knew we would, so *in advance* He arranged a rescue plan to win our love and faith and obedience. Through Christ, we win back everything we lost and more. Through Christ, we are forgiven of our terrible guilt. Through Christ, our minds are cleared of Satan's fog and our willpower is strengthened and guided. **"We love because He first loved us"** (1 John 4:19).

Q: My friend and I often debate about infant Baptism. Can little babies really have faith?

A: You wrote with a great question. The issue of infant Baptism has polarized Christians for four centuries, and as far as I can tell, the two sides are as far apart as ever. Let me attempt to summarize the Bible's words about this issue:

1. All people are sinful, little children included. They are not guiltless until an "age of accountability." The Bible says nothing about an age of accountability. What it does say, in Psalm 51:5, for example, is that people's sinfulness begins at birth, even at *conception*. Sin is a hereditary disease, and we are born addicts.

2. Baptism is pure Gospel. It is 100 percent God's gift and thus not dependent on us. Galatians 3:27 describes Baptism as something God puts on us, like a cloak of holiness to cover our sin. **"All of you who were baptized into Christ have clothed yourselves with Christ"** (NIV). It has no age restrictions—through Baptism, even newborns can receive Christ's gift of forgiveness.

3. On the day of Pentecost, Peter invited the crowd to come and be baptized **"for the forgiveness of your sins. . . . The promise is for you and for your children"** (Acts 2:38–39).

4. There is power in Baptism. Peter says in 1 Peter 3:21 that the great flood symbolizes *Baptism that now saves you.* The Bible calls it a **"washing of regeneration and renewal of the Holy Spirit"** in Titus 3:5.

5. Jesus Himself said that not only can children believe, but their simple faith is also a *model* for adults. Speaking of children, He told His proud disciples, **"For to such belongs the kingdom of God. Truly, I say to you, whoever does not receive the kingdom of God like a child shall not enter it"** (Mark 10:14–15).

6. Baptism is one of God's three ways of bringing the Gospel to people (the other two are the Word and Holy Communion). All three bring the same "I love you" message of Jesus Christ. All three can be rejected. Does Baptism guarantee that that individual will end up in heaven? No. People hear the Word and reject it and end up in hell. People hear the Word, believe it at first, and then later reject it and go to hell. People who were once baptized can later reject its promise and end up in hell. All of these "means of God's grace" can be rejected.

7. Of course, faith and repentance are important. Through Baptism, the Holy Spirit gives the power to do both. Of course, growth in the Word is important. Once a person has been baptized, that new faith needs to be nourished and fed and exercised so the dreadful outcomes in number 6 above do not happen to him or her.

Many more pages, and even entire books, have been written on this controversy. I hope you find the previous passages persuasive. But even if you don't, I hope that you will see them as an honest attempt to present what *the Bible* says, not just what denominational traditions say.

2

"Be kind to one another, tenderhearted, forgiving one another, as God in Christ forgave you." (Ephesians 4:32)

RELATIONSHIPS

Q: I know what loneliness feels like. I have six children, all grown, some married or widowed or divorced. I see them very seldom and hear from them maybe once in three months. I realize they have families and jobs and such, but all I'm asking is just a little time. I've mentioned it to them. I've mentioned how important family is, but it hasn't helped. What can I do?

A: Doesn't that story hurt your heart? I can resonate with that on both ends—I both ignore and am ignored—and my time is getting closer when I will be at home wishing my kids would call. Even now, all four of them are so caught up in their lives that they don't seem to have much time for this old boy. Kids have their own lives, and they don't feel like their parents will ever really understand them. They're very tight-lipped about all kinds of personal issues, about which they just don't want to talk to their parents. They remind me of how I was at their age.

But I also resonate with the concept of being crazy busy and not communicating. Sometimes after spending all day running around and dealing with human chaos, when I finally get home, I don't want to meet anybody else's needs. I can understand how, when your life is really a carousel, when you're running, running, running, you don't think about the someone out there who's stuck at home just wishing the phone would ring.

This viewer's question is something all of us can take to heart, reminding us to slow down our lives a little and pay attention to the people around us, especially the older ones, especially the ones who might be lonely. Communication technology has removed all of our excuses for neglecting our families.

One of the reasons God put us on this earth is to give and receive love. Not to accumulate assets and resources, not to see how many people we can get control over or how high in an organization we can be promoted. God put us here to give and receive love as our first function—first with Him, and then with one another. This letter convicts my heart. I have older relatives that I know would love to hear from me, and so today is the day I'm going to pick up the phone. Is there someone who would love to hear from you? If I do it, will you do it too?

Q: My daughter is planning a wedding for this fall. She has a concern I wasn't sure how to respond to. She was discussing the marriage vows with a friend, especially regarding the word *obey*. She feels she can't have her ceremony in the church as she doesn't agree to "obeying" her husband. She said they have many discussions because they have a two-year-old son. She said when they disagree about things, they talk through them. If they cannot agree with each other, they agree to disagree and that's the end of it. Her comment was, "If my husband told me to do something that is wrong, should I have to do it?"

A: As with any question relating to the Christian's life, the first place we need to go to is God's Word to see what He says. The marriage vows used in most Christian churches come from Ephesians 5:

> Wives, submit to your own husbands, as to the Lord. For the husband is the head of the wife even as Christ is the head of the church, His body, and is Himself its Savior. Now as the church submits to Christ, so also wives should submit in everything to their husbands. Husbands, love your wives, as Christ loved the church and gave Himself up for her, that He might sanctify her, having cleansed her by the washing of water with the word, so that He might present the church to Himself in splendor, without spot or wrinkle or any such thing, that she might be holy and without blemish. . . . Let each one of you love his wife as himself, and let the wife see that she respects her husband. (Ephesians 5:22–27,33)

The apostle Paul bases these words of encouragement to husbands and wives on Genesis 3, where God created Adam to be the head and Eve to be the helper in marriage. God established marriage and the relationship between husbands and wives *before* the fall into sin. The head/helper relationship was never a consequence of sin but was part of God's original design. Unfortunately, our sinful nature damaged God's original perfect design. In a marriage that doesn't follow God's design, the husband is a tyrant or is absent, and the wife struggles for dominance or falls into sullen submission.

In the eyes of God, men and women have equal status and equal value. That equality is guaranteed by the blood of Jesus, who has forgiven the sins of both and has made us all heirs together equally in God's family. But when God designed marriage, He chose to make the husband the *head* and the wife the *helper*. In God's world, headship is not primarily about power and authority but about taking the lead in service—loving like Jesus Christ, not like James Bond. In God's world, *helper* is not a title of inferiority but of a valuable role. In the Old Testament, the word *helper* is used seventeen times. The first two times it is used is in reference to Eve as the helper in marriage, but the other times it is used of God Himself. Helper is a high and holy calling, modeled after God's own saving help to His people.

The word *obey* in some churches' wedding vows isn't drawn from Scripture, and in today's usage it doesn't convey well what the Bible does in fact say. The word suggests a subservient, inferior position of the wife to the husband. I never used the word *obey* in the marriage services I led. In fact, even the English word *submit* is not particularly helpful today because it implies resentful, unwilling, compelled capitulation to a superior force. What Scripture actually describes for a happy marriage (and what the original Greek verb really means) is a choice that the wife makes to yield some of her independence to help build up her husband's capacity for leadership. Her yielding is chosen so the team can dance better, just as Ginger Rogers let Fred Astaire lead. *Respecting* the husband's God-given leadership is a better way to articulate the attitude God wants.

Moreover, let's not forget the high expectations God has for the husband. He is to love his wife as Christ loved the Church! No woman has to be afraid to let a man lead in the home when his model is Jesus Christ.

Q: I have great friends who are homosexual, and I don't see them as sinners. I see them as born that way. I consider myself a Christian, but my beliefs about homosexuality exclude me from many churches. What does God say about this?

A: Might I suggest that you ask God's opinion before you arrive at your own convictions? In our age of moral relativism, everybody feels licensed to publish his or her own code of behaviors, so I can understand the context of why you speak that way. But you asked the right question: What does *God* think?

He tells us. Read Romans 1. Despite better knowledge, men then and now **"gave up natural relations with women and were consumed with passion for one another, men committing shameless acts with men and receiving in themselves the due penalty for their error"** (v. 27). Practicing gays and lesbians **"will not inherit the kingdom of God"** (1 Corinthians 6:9).

That is God's view. Our society's view is that people are made that way or born that way, and since their desires and orientation are fixed, their lifestyle should be as legitimate as that of straight people. That argument, which seems plausible and broad-minded at first look, wilts under scrutiny. We would not accept the argument that someone's pedophile desires, being real and sustained, legitimize passion for sexual activity between adults and children.

We are all broken. Homosexuality is no better or worse a sin than any other, including heterosexual adultery. It's all bad. It all brings condemnation and guilt. But it has all been atoned for by the blood of Jesus. The Bible's call to repentance includes people living a gay lifestyle too. The very same chapter of the Bible that condemns unrepentant homosexuality also promises forgiveness and strength from God to people who want help in managing those desires (1 Corinthians 6:11).

I hope every Christian congregation is a safe and welcoming place where gay people can find welcome and friends. Christian churches and pastors who shun gay people only drive them deeper into the gay community for acceptance. But I also hope that every Christian congregation will provide God's clear words of judgment and restoration for people who need help escaping the trap of sexual desires God calls wrong.

Q: My son and his wife have four children, but they are currently separated because the wife is in an adulterous affair. My son, who is a Christian, has tried to get counseling for her through the church, but she has refused. He keeps hoping she will change. The problem is that he continues to visit his children three times a week at her house while she goes out with her new boyfriend. How should we as parents handle this? What does God say?

A: Ah, such pain. God's design for marriage to be a lifelong union between one man and woman is a wonderful gift. As early as Genesis 2, God said, **"A man shall leave his father and his mother and hold fast to his wife, and they shall become one flesh"** (v. 24). Unfortunately, when a husband or wife fail to live according to God's plan, a marriage can be broken. What God intends as a gift turns into heartache and pain with many casualties along the way. If there are children, they are always part of the collateral damage of a wrecked marriage.

Sadly, it sounds like the wife's adultery has broken the marriage, and it doesn't appear that she can be restored. God takes all sin seriously, whether it is adultery or anything else. However, God also loves us and never gives up on calling us to repentance. He invites all of us to come to Him and ask for His forgiveness and turn away from our sin, no matter what we've done. And you know what is so great? He forgives us because of Jesus.

I don't know why your son continues to see his children at his wife's house. Does he still love her despite her ongoing adultery? Is he trying to make things as minimally disruptive for their children as possible? Is he hoping that she will acknowledge her sin and repent of it before the divorce is final? Perhaps he is trying to stay in communication with her so she doesn't use access to the children as a weapon with which to hit him.

I know this may seem simplistic, but what your son and grandchildren need most right now is your unconditional love, listening ears, support, and prayers. Remind them that God makes new things out of broken old things and that He always works all things, even broken marriages, together for our good. People who defy God are never happy in the long run. People who faithfully and patiently do what God calls right will always prosper in the end.

Q: I have an adult son who, due to chemical dependency, is now mentally ill and may be permanently brain damaged. I'm very concerned about and grieved over his soul. What does the Bible teach us regarding mental illness in relation to salvation?

A: Tough question! What a load you carry on your heart. Here are a few thoughts. All of us, in some way, have damaged our own lives because of stupid things we've done. People damage their livers by heavy drinking; they damage or wreck relationships or their marriages by sinful actions or words; they damage relationships with their children because of emotional or physical abuse. People have been damaged by the cruelty of others in their soul and spirit. We're all the walking wounded in a way. It grieves me that your son has hurt himself so badly that his ability to reason and to think has been impaired.

But here's some good news. Our salvation, bought and paid for by Jesus Christ on His cross, is not a conditional forgiveness—it is unconditional. Faith, which connects us to Jesus Christ, is not based on our intellect or abilities. It is a gift from God, and it derives its power from the Gospel of the good news of Jesus, which is *objective*. It's something done completely by God and is *given* to us.

That forgiveness has been pronounced over the whole world, and that message of unconditional love is what persuades people to grasp it and get it. Even small children or people whose ability to reason is greatly reduced can have a simple faith. It doesn't have to be as complex and nuanced as yours. A simple, small faith in a great Savior still brings huge benefits.

Jesus once took a child and put him in front of His disciples. They had thought that Jesus' teachings were too deep for children. Jesus said that He wanted the children to come to Him. Not only *can* children believe, but their faith is also to be a *model* for adults. Do you know what that means? It is not the degree of complexity of your faith that saves you; it's not about you at all. What matters is that there is faith. Period. Even a small, childlike faith in a big Savior will be enough to bring your son the forgiveness he needs.

What you taught your son about Jesus earlier in his life might still be there in his memory. Keep telling him the simple truths of the Gospel—God's Word is powerful in its simplicity and may soak in. Has he been baptized? Baptism is an objective gift of God's forgiveness, regardless of the individual's ability to understand it. Keep praying for him—the Holy Spirit can work wonders even in the mind of someone who has suffered brain damage.

Q: While I appreciated the nod toward mothers who had both adopted and those who had placed children for adoption in your recent television message, some of your introductory remarks about the risks of adoption almost offended me. My son has always known that he was adopted, and he understands that I had prayed for a child for many years. God heard my prayer and brought me my son. I just hope your remarks don't discourage other potential adoptive families.

A: And here I thought I had given a message of encouragement about adoption. This viewer's critique reminds me how tender people are about family issues such as infertility and the stresses of adoption.

Once, on television, I told some stories about clumsy remarks I had made as a child to a neighborhood friend when I discovered that he was adopted. What I intended as a narrative of my own insensitivity was heard by this dear woman as a put-down of the whole adoptive process.

I guess there's no completely safe and painless way to talk about adoption, or for that matter, any other family issue. How can you talk about divorce as something that God doesn't want without making some already-divorced people feel bad? How can you talk about God's design for two parents in each home without making all the single parents wince and get defensive?

On the other hand, if we as Christians cannot talk about some of the risks of adoption, we're romanticizing something that inevitably has some special struggles and heartache. How could Moses not have gone through some problems with his own adoption? He was brought up in the royal court of the pharaohs of Egypt, but his own birth father probably saw him very little. He would always have felt like an outsider to some degree in the royal court. He saw his birth mom, Jochebed, a little and then not so much. She had to go through the trauma of giving her beautiful little baby to another woman, had to accept that her little Moses would call another woman "Mama."

It's realistic for us to admit that there is special pain in situations such as this. However, we need to recognize that God often gives extraordinary blessings as well. I was a foster parent for two years, and I learned a lot about that world. I don't want to overhype the foster process—some foster placements do not work out well, and fellow foster parents have relayed to me some dreadful stories of a young person and a foster couple not clicking and having to move on, amidst brokenness and hard feelings. Foster parenting doesn't fix everything. Nevertheless, it usually succeeds in its primary mission: it brings stabilization into the life of a kid in crisis.

Moses' own adoption turned out to have extraordinary benefits for God's plan of salvation. He became familiar with the ways of the royal court of the pharaohs where, as an eighty-year-old man, he would appear as leader of the Israelite nation. He could speak their language; he could write their hieroglyphic writing. Think of the executive training he received as he watched Pharaoh and the Egyptian senior leadership work at solving problems in their huge country. God was training Moses five decades in advance for executive leadership over Israel.

If you yourself were adopted or if you have an adopted child or someone in your family is adopted or you have friends that either were adopted or chose to adopt, I hope you are always looking for the special and extraordinary blessings that God can bring into your life, just as He did in the life of Moses. I hope you will admire the courage of people who grow up in an adoptive situation and the courage of people who take a child into their home, knowing the risks. I hope you will salute the courage of mothers who, like Jochebed, are willing to sacrifice their feelings and give up their children in order to make a better life for them.

Q: How should I respond to my friends who think living together before marriage is a good way to "try out" marriage to see if it will work for them?

A: Ask them: Whose approval do you most desire in life? Your friends'? Your boyfriend's? Your parents'? Or, dare I say it, God's?

Satan owns the short term. Nobody can compete with the immediate rewards of the tempter. Sexuality outside of marriage—the Bible calls it adultery—always brings excitement, risk, danger, adventure, and no commitment. But Satan cannot deliver satisfaction, happiness of heart, joy, contentment, or peace. No matter how we try to dance around it, rationalize it, contextualize it, or compare ourselves to other people, sex outside marriage is adultery and adultery is sin. Sin always leaves us with guilt; guilt always poisons the long-term experience.

God wants us to have sex. He invented it to bring joy into our lives. But its misuse causes great social havoc, from unwanted children to abortion to sexually transmitted diseases. If you are interested in God's approval, listen up: **"Let marriage be held in honor among all, and let the marriage bed be undefiled, for God will judge the sexually immoral and adulterous"** (Hebrews 13:4). Sex without a permanent commitment will hurt both people.

Think of it like this: Don't you have enough problems without having God against you too? Wouldn't you rather have the power source of the universe making things work for you instead of making things unravel? Who needs more guilt? Marriage is not slavery. It is a committed partnership in which sexuality can flourish without doing damage and without a guilt hangover.

Q: I got divorced by my choice ten years ago and remarried two years later. Was it wrong in God's eyes for me to remarry? Is it considered adultery? I feel a lot of guilt about my current marriage, like it's not God-pleasing. I know God forgives our sins, but I don't feel forgiven.

A: There really are two questions here: Was it right to divorce, and was it right to remarry?

First, the divorce. You said it was by your choice. Does that mean you broke up the marriage or that your partner's evils were so great that you couldn't stand it anymore? God is on record as hating divorce. His intent is that marriage lasts till death us do part. His intent is a one-flesh commitment that belongs to Him, a commitment that nobody should break apart.

The Bible reveals only two exceptions when a Christian may seek a divorce without sinning. One is adultery by your partner (Matthew 19:9) and the other is when you are married to an unbeliever and he or she leaves the marriage (1 Corinthians 7:15). If one of these two exceptions applies to your situation, you bear no guilt for the breakup.

If the breakup was your fault, a heart of true repentance would have led you to do whatever you could to restore the relationship. Getting a counselor or pastor to help the reconciliation process is always a good idea.

But sometimes reconciliation is impossible—the former spouse isn't interested, or one or both of you have remarried. Then it's time to pack up and move on. True repentance means that you acknowledge your own sinful faults in the breakup, do what you can to help with the collateral damage (children, property, reputation, and so on), claim the forgiveness that Jesus bought, and pray for strength to go forward and live right.

Now, the second part—were you in the clear to remarry? Some of the English translations of the New Testament have a slightly confusing mistranslation in several passages, including Matthew 5:32, part of Jesus' famous Sermon on the Mount: **"Everyone who divorces his wife, except on the ground of sexual immorality, makes her commit adultery, and whoever marries a divorced woman commits adultery."**

A more precise and careful translation would note some subtleties in the Greek grammar of Matthew's original and would go like this: "Everyone who divorces his wife, except on the ground of sexual immorality, *causes her to be regarded as an adulteress,* and whoever marries a divorced woman *is regarded as an adulterer."* Read in context, Jesus' words are a gentle discouragement of divorce, not a condemnation of divorcees who remarry.

The bottom line? You are now married to a new spouse. Go forward with all your heart and commit yourself 100 percent. Bathe each day in Jesus' forgiveness for your past sins and pray for the Spirit's wisdom and strength to live happily ever after in this new relationship.

Q: How does God feel about birth control? I have heard many Christians say God gives us free will to choose how many children we want. Is birth control just an early form of abortion—giving back God's blessings, telling Him, "No thanks"? God is in charge of life; do we have the right to prevent it?

A: Birth control is one of those adiaphora, that is, something that God neither forbids nor commands in the Bible. He leaves these decisions to your good judgment.

What God does tell us is that children are a great blessing from Him (Psalm 127) and He doesn't want us to view them as a social or financial disaster. Birth control, however, is not abortion (the

RU-486 pill excepted). Avoiding conception is not the moral equivalent of killing an unborn baby.

There is nothing in the Bible that obligates you to generate as many children as you can, just as marriage is a great blessing but single people are not obligated to be married to please God. God is indeed in charge of creating life, but He gives you and me major partnership roles in how those blessings come to pass. My counsel to you is to get in a three-way huddle in prayer with your spouse and with God and work out your family plan.

Q: God says, "Be fruitful and multiply." Does that mean my wife and I must have kids? We aren't sure about raising kids in the world as it is.

A: See the answer to the previous question. God's words to Adam and Eve in Genesis 1:28 are not a law mandating certain behaviors and threatening punishment if you disobey. They are an empowering commission and promise. They are His blessing of pro-creative power. They declare a reproductive partnership between God and humankind that makes possible the greatest miracle I have ever seen: the birth of a child. "Be fruitful" is not a law.

But having said that, it is good to examine your rationale for not wanting to produce children. Is it because you want to adopt, opening your arms for children who might be unloved and unwanted somewhere else? That would be awesome. Is it because you think our world is so rotten and corrupt that you would fear for their survival? That attitude would seem to be telling God that His arms are too short to take care of His business. Is it because in today's economy you aren't sure you can afford them? God will find a way to help you feed, clothe, and educate your children.

The wicked world we live in desperately needs Christians who step up and get involved, not who run away or hide somewhere or disengage. One of the greatest legacies that a Christian couple can leave to posterity is children who will keep the family's Christian witness alive.

Q: I am constantly worrying about my children and my husband. My husband says I need to relax and trust that God is in control. I just can't help myself. How can I let go of the fear?

A: Make sure you know the difference between concern and worry. Concern is good, and wives and mothers bring huge value to the family because they think of things and remember things that dads and kids forget. Mother-sense has spared people much misery. Planning, forethought, organization, and alertness are all valuable, and I'll bet that you're good at all of those things.

Worry is sin, however, because worry is fear. Fear that everything is right on the edge of unraveling. Fear that we won't have enough. Fear that my spouse will abandon me any day now. Fear that people hate me. Fear that my children secretly despise me. Fear of what other people are saying about me.

Since your husband probably doesn't feel things the way you do, take time to help him understand your vulnerability. Perhaps you are so insecure about yourself that you feel weak all the time. Help him understand how much you crave his words of assurance, his words of praise and appreciation, and his steady handling of family stress.

Get to know God's assurance passages in Scripture. Can you recite the end of Matthew 6 by heart? Jesus Himself speaks these comforting words: **"I tell you, do not be anxious about your life, what you will eat or what you will drink, nor about your body,**

what you will put on. . . . Look at the birds of the air: they neither sow nor reap nor gather into barns, and yet your heavenly Father feeds them. Are you not of more value than they?" (Matthew 6:25–26).

Hold tight to Jesus' promise never to leave you or forsake you. To Him you are precious and valuable!

Q: My mother-in-law is a terrible gossip, constantly "filling me in" on what's going on with others in the family. I shudder to think what she says about me! How do I encourage her to stop without being disrespectful?

A: First off, we have to define what we mean by "gossip." One of my dearest and oldest friends could yak your ears off and wanted to know absolutely everything going on with everybody. She used to say, "It's not gossip—it's just news about friends." Perhaps not everything your mother-in-law tells you is evil or slanderous. Perhaps she is just caught up in the stories of how everybody she cares about is doing.

Gossip, however, is more than just news about friends. Gossip

- repeats things that aren't true;
- shares information that ruins other people's reputations;
- enjoys other people's pain; and
- prolongs a conflict that could be healed.

When she strays into those areas, stop the conversation and establish boundaries. Steer the conversation into gossip's opposite— "building-up talk":

- finding things to praise about people;
- clapping and cheering for others' successes;

- praying for people who are struggling; and
- paying attention to the fears and insecurities of the person talking.

Q: My nephew is a very difficult and spoiled child. Sometimes I think he needs a good spanking, but my sister doesn't "believe" in spanking. Does the Bible say anything about disciplining children?

A: It does indeed. The Book of Proverbs contains quite a few passages, including **"Whoever spares the rod hates his son, but he who loves him is diligent to discipline him"** (13:24) or **"The rod and reproof give wisdom, but a child left to himself brings shame to his mother"** (29:15). Of the Ten Commandments, numbers 4 through 10 govern human relationships, and the first one of these God mentions is "Honor your father and your mother."

Note a few things, however, especially you corporal punishment enthusiasts. The word *spank* (meaning to strike with the flat of the hand upon the gluteus maximus of the offender) does not show up in the Bible. The Proverbs passages use the word *rod*. May I speak frankly? I do not know a single person, Christian or non-Christian, who strikes his or her children with sticks.

It is a feature of our age to discover grotesque stories of physical abuse that children have endured at the hands of those who were supposed to protect and educate them. People of our age have become unusually sensitive to how children are treated. In the span of my parish ministry, parochial schoolteachers have had to change their discipline methods considerably. I know of two who lost their positions because of the way in which they used their hands on disobedient children. I will identify myself as a spanker of my own children, but I note (as do other tough parents like me) that we spanked our last-born child a whole lot less than the firstborn. My wife and I got quite a bit of mileage out of time-out chairs and withdrawal of privileges.

What is not negotiable is that parents (and grandparents and teachers) absolutely must train children to obey their adult leaders. They must mean what they say and expect an appropriate response the first time. Children who have not learned to obey their parents will probably not respect their teachers either, and they may turn out to be poor employment risks because they can't submit to a boss's direction.

Q: My father left my family when I was young. Now I'm a father, but I don't know how to guide my children because I never had a good role model. Can you point me to some Scripture that will help me?

A: Great question, and very self-aware. My first suggestion is for you to identify some role models and mentors in your circle of family and friends. Find a guy (age irrelevant) who has a happy wife and whose kids you think turned out pretty well. Humble yourself and get him talking about his philosophy of marriage and child rearing. Ask if you can call him when you have a dilemma.

Now, here are a few Scripture passages that speak to your question:

1. **"Husbands, love your wives, as Christ loved the church and gave Himself up for her"** (Ephesians 5:25). It is a great thing when children see their fathers respecting and

protecting and loving their mother. Don't ever argue or fight with her in front of them. Work out your problems behind a closed door.

2. **"Blessed is everyone who fears the LORD, who walks in His ways! You shall eat the fruit of the labor of your hands; you shall be blessed, and it shall be well with you. Your wife will be like a fruitful vine within your house; your children will be like olive shoots around your table. Behold, thus shall the man be blessed who fears the LORD"** (Psalm 128:1–4). When you prize your relationship with the Lord and make His Word and His house and His worship high priorities, everything else falls into place. Everything works.

3. **"Fathers, do not provoke your children to anger, but bring them up in the discipline and instruction of the Lord"** (Ephesians 6:4). Some men think that child rearing is a woman's job. God thinks the buck stops with you.

Here are a few nuggets I've learned from good dads I have observed:

- You are not your kids' buddy or peer. You can play with them, wrestle with them, and watch football with them, but you will always be above them. When you give an order, give it once, once only, and expect to be obeyed.

- Don't promise anything on which you don't fully intend to follow through. Keep every promise. Don't overpromise or use promises as a cheap way to get them to be quiet.

- As they get older, they will need you less and less to tell them what to do and more and more to listen to them.

Q: Forgiving and forgetting is often hard. How can we forgive people using Jesus' example?

A: Forgiving the other sinners around us isn't often hard; it's always hard. We're sinners too. Forgiving others, though, is not optional for Christians. In very strong language, the Lord Jesus told us that withholding forgiveness to our debtors would threaten our own forgiveness from God.

I think one of the keys is to get rid of the horrible phrase "forgive and forget." We can't control our memories as though they are computer files that we can simply delete at will. The real challenge for us as Christians is to forgive while remembering.

The fuel that our hearts need to let go of hurt and anger comes from Christ. How great are our own sins against Him. How great is His Gospel love for us that He chose to forgive us even before we were born. How patient is His love to keep forgiving us even though we often repeat the same sins over and over.

The more we are conscious of Christ's forgiveness toward us, the kinder we can be toward those who sin against us. When people say "I'm sorry" to us, we can gently and graciously say forgiving words. But even when they don't appear to be repentant, we can choose to let go of our bitterness and anger. **"I can do all things through Him who strengthens me"** (Philippians 4:13).

Q: A well-loved young man from our town was killed in Iraq. Many people from the town are bitter and feel that if he had not been in Iraq, he would still be alive. How can I offer comfort to those who feel like this? Did God cause his death?

A: We need to be careful neither to overstate nor to understate hope for people in grief such as this. Psalm 139 shows us that God sees all of a person's life and knows us backward and forward. In that sense, God could see this soldier's whole life trajectory at birth as though it had already happened.

And yet, the Bible does not teach that God controls all of human life like a puppeteer. The ancient Greeks and Romans were fatalists: that is, they believed that all human life was measured and then cut by three all-powerful and mysterious women (the "Fates"). Although nobody today really believes in the secret workings of Clotho the spinner, Lachesis the measurer, and Atropos the cutter, we still use fatalist talk, assuming that things are "destined," "fated," "doomed," "meant to be." Millions of people believe that our lives are controlled by the power of the stars and their relative positions in the sky, and they devour daily horoscopes and try to find the secrets of that celestial influence. People today really believe that Romeo and Juliet were "star-crossed" lovers.

The Bible teaches that God has all things under His watch and control, and that He has ordained certain things to be. But it is simultaneously true that He chooses to interact with us and allows us a measure of independence. Our choices and words and actions do matter. We are not just His hand puppets or marionettes on His strings. He has created us to be junior versions of Himself, choosing what is right and rejecting what is evil. Through Christ's forgiveness and the indwelling of the Holy Spirit, guided by His Word, we have regained the image of God, and it is the Spirit's lifework within us to grow us into the fullness of that wonderful new identity.

Q: Recently, you did a series about relationships. You covered ways that women do wrong by their husbands, but your solution to the problem left me wanting more. You said, "A better way [to treat your husband] is to make him big so he lives up to your expectations, to build him up." I want to build my husband up, but I don't know how. Do you have any suggestions?

A: Many wives realize after some years of marriage that they are not married to Prince Charming. In their disappointment, they see in their husband only the many ways in which he is a letdown, and they become blind and mute about his good qualities. If my wife sat down with a legal pad, she could have the first page of complaints and faults about me written up without even breaking into a sweat.

Love him the way Christ loves you—unconditionally and freely. Respect him as you respect Christ. We men would like love from our women, but we cannot live without their respect. It is oxygen for our souls. If we don't feel like a leader in our homes, we will happily ditch the job and let the woman do it. Some of us men wouldn't mind at all regressing to acting like boys again. If we are treated like children, we will act like children.

Your husband has good qualities. Take some time to reflect and list them. Let your mind dwell on them instead of on his faults. Let him know that you see and appreciate what he does to support and help the family. What things would you miss most if you were a widow? Tell him. Make your voice say those things out loud, without attaching criticisms at the end. Without attaching a "but" clause. Without comparing him to the man you wish he were.

Ever hear the phrase, "You can attract more flies with honey than vinegar"? Men have many, many faults, but women do too, and one of them can be to reach too quickly for the sharp or whiny voice that drives us away. Use the nuclear option of sexual deprivation only in the most extreme and desperate of situations. Identify for yourself the qualities in him that drew you to him in the first place. Praise him for those things, and he will aspire to act like that more.

✳✳

Q: I have a friend who is dabbling in Buddhism. I have shared my faith in Jesus with her and have even shared some of your materials. I don't feel like I'm getting through. What can I do?

A: We never know for sure which of our words are getting through. And we don't need to know—it's not our business. It's our job just to tell the truth: that we are condemned sinners but that Jesus accepted our condemnation, suffered, died, and rose again to give us forgiveness. No one, Buddhists included, can get rid of guilt on his or her own. You can assume that your friend feels guilt. The great news of Christ is true, and its message has power to cut right through to a person's heart.

People are funny. We don't like to get pushed around by others, and letting someone else change our way of thinking is not easy. We may be changing our minds, but we don't want to show it. We don't want to look weak or dumb. Be patient—think long term.

Just speak the truth in love to your friend. Listen first; speak later. Keep your voice soft and your hopes high.

✳✳

Q: How do I confront my friend with her sinful behavior without being perceived as self-righteous or, because she's my friend, lowering the bar to accept her behavior?

A: You have described the situation elegantly. It is a dilemma that many of us face with friends and even close family. I think the correct answer is to do your best at both.

God's Word in 1 Peter 3:15–16 has some good advice for us. God does indeed want His believers to be His witnesses. We are God's voice and hands in our communities. We are His royal ambassadors to a dying planet. Here are some key points:

- Just tell the truth. You don't have to argue with people. You don't have to try to make the words palatable in today's culture. Just tell the truth. It's not your message. It's God's. Back it up with Scripture so it's clear that it's not just your opinion.

- If you are rejected, don't take it personally. It's God with whom they have a problem, not you.

- Speak humbly. You also are a starving beggar whom God has loved and fed and clothed.

- Speak the truth with gentleness and respect.

- Let the person know you will always love him or her. Don't punish a sinner with shunning.

- People hate to seem weak by backing down easily. They may need time to change their minds and hearts. Tell the truth and then back off and let them think. It's God's power that will change people, not yours.

Q: When someone doesn't want you to write or speak to him or her about Jesus, should you stay away from that person?

A: When you are hoping to be able to connect and communicate with someone who looks and talks like an unbeliever or whose faith seems to you to be slipping away, it may seem as though you have no chance and no power. When someone is defiantly atheistic or agnostic, things can look pretty bleak. But shunning them or avoiding them will only make matters worse. Then there's one less Christian person in his or her life.

Remember that you have two very powerful things with which to work. The first is guilt in that person's heart. You can deny it, ignore it, sedate it with drugs and alcohol, rationalize it, explain it away, distract yourself, and blame others, but you can get rid of guilt only through faith in the blood of Jesus.

The second power at your disposal is the unshakable truth of God's Word. It is true even when someone else denies it, and it cuts right to the bone, as the Book of Hebrews says (4:12). Be brief in your spiritual messages. When you tell God's truth, your words will stick deep, even when a person is in denial. Perhaps the person will remember later what you said.

In the meantime, stay close and be a friend. When you are a true friend, you earn the right to be listened to. Treat other people, especially unbelievers, with the same unconditional love that Jesus Christ shows toward you.

Q: Is it ever okay for us as Christians to judge others?

A: Now there's a loaded question, and it needs both a no and a yes. Nobody wants to be described with the adjective *judgmental* today, isn't it so? Most people, even non-Bible readers, can quote Jesus' words from the Sermon on the Mount: **"Do not judge, or you too will be judged"** (Matthew 7:1 NIV).

So what is Jesus condemning in that verse?

- Feeling superior to others; imagining that you are more worthy of God's approval; despising another person.

- Enjoying making other people squirm by manipulating their guilty consciences.

- Being quick to criticize but slow to forgive and show mercy.

- Making up and imposing more spiritual laws and rules than God Himself has.

On the other hand, that doesn't mean that you may never point out wrong beliefs or sinful actions in other people. You have God's permission, even a duty, to be involved in the lives of people around you. St. Paul writes in Galatians 6:1, **"Brothers, if anyone is caught in any transgression, you who are spiritual should restore him in a spirit of gentleness."**

So what is Paul encouraging?

- Restoring, not condemning.

- Speaking the truth, but speaking gently, in love.

- Speaking humbly, knowing that you need God's mercy too.

- Speaking with the goal of lifting someone up, not beating him or her down.

Q: How should we communicate with our grandchildren and great-grandchildren so we can give them good Christian advice but not have them ignore us or turn a deaf ear?

A: Older people often feel hurt in talking about important things with younger people, because one of the conceits of youth is that they think they know it all. Actually, I think they do listen and remember if we "elders" come in the right spirit and tone. Try these steps:

Love unconditionally. Even when they are living in a way we (and the Bible) consider immoral, the debt of love we owe others, especially our family, is always with us.

Listen to their stories, points of view, and troubles. You may have to ask often, wait for answers, and really show you're committed and interested, because teens especially think their world is so different from yours that your input is useless to them.

Respect their right to make their own choices. If you sound like you're trying to push them around, they will do the opposite just to prove a point.

Be patient. Personal spiritual growth is never rapid. Maturity (including your own) comes over the course of years. Remember how patient God has been with you.

Q: My teenage son is depressed. He says that things never go right for him. He is even questioning his faith and wonders if there is any meaning or point to his life. How do I talk to him about this? What do I do?

A: My wife, Carol, and I have graduated from the hard school of being parents of three teenagers, and we are finishing up with number four. Here are some thoughts, not necessarily in order of importance:

1. Kids go through stages where they try on different masks and philosophies. Teenager philosophy is very fluid. Kids change their ideas like changing jeans. It is possible that your son won't think like this next year.

2. There is often a subtext to what people say. Your son's words might be code for one of the following:

- I feel blue.

- I don't know if I have any friends. Does anybody like me?

- I see myself as a failure.

- I prayed for some things that are important to me and God didn't make them happen. Now I'm afraid to trust Him with my dreams.

- Making my way in a big, nasty world seems overwhelming. I'm scared to have to navigate the adult world by myself.

3. The actual answer to his question about meaning is that God has not only bought us forgiveness so that we can pass the judgment and go to heaven, but He has also given us the great honor and dignity to be His critically important teammates in rescuing other human beings from Satan's snares and traps. Your son's life matters a great deal—he will have a sphere of influence in life that nobody else will. He is uniquely positioned to make a difference in people's lives.

4. When I counsel people with depression, I have found that the last thing they need is a scolding, law, or pressure. They already feel bad inside. What they need is

a. patience as they work through their fears and confusion;

b. steady, unconditional love; and

c. an invitation to be part of a team that serves others. When people find their mental world turning in on itself, when they think only about their own pain or despair, it becomes a bottomless pit. The best way to lift people's spirits is to help them help somebody else.

3

"Go . . . and make disciples of all nations." (Matthew 28:19)

WITNESSING

Q: My unchurched neighbor and I are friends, but I struggle with bringing up the subject of religion. I feel like I'm slotting it into a conversation and it seems out of place. How can I do it more smoothly?

A: Great question—that is a challenge. Because all of us have to protect ourselves against the massive onslaught of advertising and marketing each day, we all have developed formidable sales-resistance armor. For another thing, not all the Christians in mass media have made Christianity look good. Here are a few thoughts:

1. Take the time to demonstrate that you genuinely care about your neighbor and his or her family. Establish yourself as a good and real listener before you launch into any serious Jesus talking.

2. Listen for cues and hints of pain and brokenness. Everybody is wounded. When your neighbor trusts you enough to share pain stories, that may be permission for you to offer some healing. Listen for opportunities to offer to pray for him or her.

3. Your short-term objective should not be to straighten out your neighbor's wrong religious opinions or to get him or her to join your organization. Your short-term goal is to be ready for opportunities to connect your friend with God's Word.

4. Your neighbor can be a guest in your home when you have other Christians over and there is more overt Christian talk. Everybody craves love and acceptance, and in a cruel, dog-eat-dog world, when "outsiders" see genuine affection and real relationships, it will make your Jesus talk more natural and believable.

5. You can give your neighbor something small to read—a booklet or Web site—so he or she can feel free to pursue it privately without your standing right there. People aren't eager to have their whole life philosophy challenged by a semistranger. They don't want to feel pushed around. They want to feel as though they are choosing.

Q: "One big problem that I see in our country is a need for Christian *confrontation*," reads one of the letters I received. "People need to adhere to a scriptural code of behavior. Too many of us fail to *confront* folks that we know who are living together without being married. Too many of us fail to talk to our neighbors and friends who take Sunday as a day off, rather than to attend church to hear of their need for a Savior or feed their faith. In this way, their lives are weakened by spiritual neglect."

A: There's more, but you get the point. Is this an important part of our Christian life, that we *confront* things around us that are not right, not godly, and not scriptural?

The major issue is whether or not your discussion is with a believer in Christ. If you suspect that the person is not a believer, or he or she doesn't show any traces of active Christianity, your primary goal is not to change immoral behaviors but to get the person connected to the Gospel of Christ. One of the primary purposes of the Bible is as a mirror in which we see our sin and, therefore, our need for Jesus. See the previous question and some that follow for strategic thinking on basic evangelistic witnessing.

When a friend or family member is a Christian, however, and is exhibiting immoral behaviors, a different approach is called for. Take a look at Galatians 6. St. Paul talks about not only the *permission* but even the *obligation* for people to be involved in the behavior of the lives of Christian people around us because of what's at stake. Not only does unrepented sin have a corrosive effect on saving faith, but Christians living in unrepented sin also give a terrible and even hypocritical witness to the world and can make Jesus look bad.

Here's what Paul wrote in Galatians: **"Brothers, if anyone is caught in any transgression, you who are spiritual should restore him in a spirit of gentleness."** Note the word *gentleness*. **"Keep watch on yourself, lest you too be tempted"** (6:1). See that? No hypocrisy. You may be just as much in need of being straightened out as the person to whom you're talking. Jesus had strong words about being aware of the log in your own eye before you attempt a speckectomy on your friend.

"Bear one another's burdens, and so fulfill the law of Christ. For if anyone thinks he is something, when he is nothing, he deceives himself" (6:2–3). If we are to have any success in helping someone else change sinful behaviors, that person must hear a humble voice from a heart that says, "I'm no better than you—I need Jesus' love and forgiveness as much as you do." Humility in this conversation is not merely nice; it is imperative. Your words about changes in someone's life will be better received if you say them while helping that person carry her burdens.

"Let each one test his own work, and then his reason to boast will be in himself alone and not in his neighbor. For each will have to bear his own load" (6:4–5). The whole point of being willing to say something difficult or confrontational to someone else is not for keeping score. It's not to help you feel better about yourself; it's not to look down on someone else; it's not to take out the trash of the world around you, to try to clean things up in your visual environment. The only reason that God would allow you to speak for Him in this way is to help another sinner escape spiritual destruction, the same destruction you deserve but were spared from by the death and resurrection of Jesus Christ.

So how do you do that? First of all, make sure that you yourself come with an attitude of humility, that you yourself are mindful and repentant of your own sin. You need a Savior, Jesus Christ, as much as anybody does in the world around you. Second, you better know what you're talking about. It will not do simply to repeat slogans and clichés from past societal expectations, let's say of the way America *used to be.*

You need to be in your Bible enough to know what you're talking about. If you're going to lay a message on somebody that his or her life is not right, you better know where to find that message in Scripture. Nobody will change his or her life just because of pressure from you. In fact, most people hate pressure from others and will push back and do the opposite. You can see that in teen behavior—teenagers often contradict their parents even when they know their parents are right, simply because they don't want to feel like they're getting pushed around. So they do the opposite to make a point, even though it's wrong and stupid and hurtful in the long run.

This discussion always needs to be framed by asking "What has God said?" so that if the individual has a problem with what you're saying, the problem is not with you. The problem, ultimately, is with God. Ultimately, only God's clear words can convict a person of knowing something's wrong; only God's kindness and love can melt an icy human heart; only the Gospel can inspire a person to want to choose to do what is right.

Essentially, Jesus said in Matthew 7, "When you do that, don't judge." Judging means, "I think I'm better than you." Judging means, "I kind of enjoy putting you down and keeping score." Judging means, "I can't see my own weaknesses, but I sure can see yours." Judging means that you seem to enjoy bossing people around or are proud of your moral superiority. None of that has any place in this discussion.

The great danger is that if people are *trapped* in a sin, *addicted* to rebellion against God, they will also stop believing in God's Law and His Gospel, His words of accountability and His rescue. Unrepented sin destroys saving faith over time. But there's hope—when believers speak the truth in love, restoration is possible. **"Restore him in a spirit of gentleness"** (Galatians 6:1).

Q: For many years, I've wondered if I was doing enough witnessing and evangelism. I would think, "What can I do?" I have this great gift to share and I don't know how to. Then I realized that by supporting your ministry, I am helping to share. Maybe I can't give thousands of dollars, but with what I can afford, along with the most powerful thing I can give—prayer—I am making a difference.

A: Well, what a great question and kind words. I've got two answers for you.

First, through the magic of television and a mass media outreach such as *Time of Grace* (which depends not just on me, but on the thousands and thousands of people who hold it together and support it financially), we really are able to throw our Gospel voice all over the country and all over the globe. When you become a *Time of Grace* partner, when you pray for me to gain divine help to hold me up and help me keep it together, when you pray for God's blessings upon me, when you make a contribution that supports our purchase of airtime, then my voice becomes your voice. Together we are answering the Great Commission of Jesus to make disciples of all nations.

However, I also want you to know that your own personal witness is really important. God has put you in a situation where you have a circle of influence. These are people who hear your witness. Everybody has a circle or a sphere of influence of people who will listen to him or her. Perhaps others don't always show that they're listening, but they will remember and hear what you say. So it is important for you to develop your own capacity to talk about the Lord Jesus in a real and personal way. You don't have to try to sound like me or any other pastor. You don't have to try to sound like a television evangelist or a theology professor. You just need to sound like you.

I have some words of encouragement for you from 1 Peter 3. In verse 15, he gives what I think is the most beautiful, sweet, and concise how-to on witnessing in the entire Bible. He says this: **"In your hearts set apart Christ as Lord"** (NIV).

You can't testify to your faith if it isn't real. **"Set apart Christ as Lord"** means making sure Jesus really is at the center of your life. Your example of living is not a testimony in itself. That needs words. But the way in which you live will give an indication to the people around you whether to take your words seriously and whether your faith seems like it's for real or not.

What does this "setting apart" look like? It means seeing yourself as accountable to Christ the Creator. It means repenting of the sins that make you guilty before Christ the Judge. It means believing the message of forgiveness from Christ the Crucified. It means kneeling in worship before Christ the Savior. It means placing yourself under the command of Christ the Lord.

Next, **"always [be prepared] to make a defense to anyone who asks you for a reason for the hope that is in you."** Being prepared means that in order to be able to give a coherent explana-tion of God's rescue plan, you have to know it yourself. Get into your Bible and know what God has been up to in human history. Know what He has done on your behalf. Then be prepared to tell it back in terms that make sense to you (after you have first explained it to yourself) until your own questions have been answered. Tell what you know.

"Yet do it with gentleness and respect." We often hear things that other people say about religion or God or even the Bible that sound ridiculous or we know to be false. But people come to the Lord in all different stages of life, and they're at many different points in their relationship with Him and in the development of their faith. Even if they may have lived for many decades, they may be way be-hind in spiritual knowledge.

When you listen to people, you don't need to put down the things they're saying that you know are wrong. You don't have to criticize them; you don't have to appear to be judging them or con-demning them. Just be positive and tell the truth. Speak gently, speak clearly, and testify more to what the Lord Jesus has done than to showing the contradictions or ridiculing the foolishness of what you may hear people say.

Speak these things **"with gentleness and respect."** You are sharing the Word of Life. You're not talking down to people; you're not belittling them or patronizing them. You're sharing from one beggar to another; you're sharing the beautiful bread of the Lord Jesus, the bread of life, the food that makes us alive.

When you share the things that you have come to believe and know from Scripture, do it *gently*, with soft words, and do it with *respect*, not shoving anything down anyone's throat. Put it out there with respect for someone to think about, and then let it go. It's the power *in those very words* that will change someone else's heart, not necessarily the great skill in which you lay it out there or how eloquent and flowery your words can be or how intense or hard-hitting you are. None of that is really going to make any difference because the power is in the words themselves—words from God.

Q: My children love to tell others about Jesus. But they don't understand why sometimes their witnessing seems to be ignored or even made fun of by other kids. They can't understand why anyone wouldn't believe in Jesus. How can I encourage them?

A: You can help them by framing this activity in terms of a war, which in fact it is. We are at war with Satan and his demons, and they are everywhere. Satan will never give up his grip on people's hearts without a fight. People are proud, and they don't easily admit that they need help.

You can help your kids thank God that they were brought up in the faith from early on—imagine how strange the Bible's message must sound to people who never heard the stories. In my opinion, the older you get, the harder it is to become a believer, because you have so many more distractions, so many more objections, so many more skills in evasion and pretense.

You can help your kids to believe that a relationship with Christ really satisfies, really meets our needs in the end. Everyone fears death; only Christ gives us solid hope of forgiveness in the judgment and life after death.

The world of business and schoolyards can be hard, cruel places, full of cheating and betrayals. Everybody craves a place of acceptance, genuine love and care, and significance. You can help your kids to believe that the loving relationships people can find in a Christian congregation make church a great place to be. Perhaps when their playground friends are guests in your home and hear you pray, see you love one another, and sense your cohesion, they will find things to admire.

Q: Why does witnessing for our faith make so many Christians uncomfortable?

A: It is easy for us to slide into a mode of being simply passive consumers of religious services, customers only. After all, that's why we rent the clergy, isn't it? They do the talking, and we sit there and listen and get what we need and then go home. You've heard of couch potatoes? Well, it's easy to stay pew potatoes.

- If you feel like a rookie in your faith, you might not feel qualified to talk to someone else.
- If you have some major messes in your life, you might feel like a hypocrite talking to another sinner.
- If your life already seems full with work and home and family duties, it may seem as if there's no time to reach out to someone else.
- Doing anything for the first time is like jumping over a high hurdle—you're afraid of tripping and scraping up your knees and face.

Do it anyway. Be uncomfortable for Jesus. It works. You'll get better at it.

Q: I often feel weak and confused in my own faith. Am I of any use? Does Jesus really need little me?

A: The power to bring change to another person's mind and heart doesn't come from you. It comes from the Word of God. The Bible calls itself both a sharp sword to reveal human guilt and a soothing balm to bring healing to spiritual wounds. When you simply speak God's words, you are bringing God's wisdom and power. Jesus said in Matthew 5, **"You are the salt of the earth"** and **"You are the light of the world"** (vv. 13–14). It's true—when you were baptized, you were not only adopted into God's family but also drafted into His army. It's not a question of whether or not you are a minister for Him in your life. It's only a matter of what kind of minister you will be.

Christianity is not merely one of the world religions that people in their hunger for the divine have constructed to help soothe their way through life. It quite literally is life or death. Will people spend eternity in great joy with the Maker of the world or spend eternity receiving punishment for having joined the rebellion against God? You are part of the rescue process.

St. Paul has encouragement for little you to step up to your high calling, claim your royal identity, and gain some self-confidence: **"I myself am satisfied about you, my brothers, that you yourselves are full of goodness, filled with all knowledge and able to instruct one another"** (Romans 15:14). That is to say, you have good hearts. You know enough to get started. You already possess sufficient communication skills. Let's go!

Q: How can I summarize the Christian message?

A: I have a little memory device: I call it the "Four Key Words." SIN—GRACE—FAITH—WORKS. You must tell the story in that order.

- Tell people about their **sin**—the dreadful curses that come from human rebellion: pain during our lives, the death of our bodies, and condemnation in eternity.

- Tell people about God's **grace**—His decision to love us anyway, unconditionally; God's Son, Jesus, came to earth as God and man, relived our lives for us, suffered our death, and rose again to reconcile the whole world to God.

- Tell people about **faith**—that all of the benefits of Christ's forgiveness come to us through believing in it.

- Tell people about **works**—that God calls you to live a new life, not in order to be saved but because you have been saved. Make sure this comes last; our lives of faith and service are a response to our salvation, not the cause of our salvation.

Q: What's the best way to share the Gospel with an unbeliever?

A: There is no one best way. But here are a few timeless principles of Christian communication:

- Build a relationship first. People need to know that you care about them whether or not they end up joining your organization.

- Read 1 Peter 3 (as mentioned earlier in this section). Whenever you speak, do it with gentleness and respect. When people have not grown up in God's Word, of course their spiritual ideas will often sound ridiculous. Be patient. Use a soft voice.

- Be yourself. Don't try to pretend to be someone else. You are a worthy sharer of the Gospel just as you are.

- Don't be afraid to say, "I don't know, but I'll get back to you."

- Listen first and ask lots of questions before you launch into your persuasion talk.

- Invite people to come with you to worship, to a Bible study, to read Christian materials, to watch Christian videos, or to check out a Christian Web site. It's scary to go it alone. Walk with them to the degree they let you.

Q: It seems like in our society, embracing all faiths is the "in" thing. "Whatever you believe is okay with me, as long as it doesn't interfere with my beliefs." Christ as the *only way* to heaven is viewed as close-minded and exclusionary. How can we as Christians get through to those with that view?

A: What you are observing is happening more and more. It is fashionable today not to view truth as absolute but rather as relative. "Your truth" is for you, and "my truth" works for me.

That's pure baloney, of course. There aren't two or more equally valid ways to compute arithmetic problems. Neither are there two or more ways to acceptance by God. Just tell the truth. Christianity is first of all *inclusive:* God's grace is for all. God in Christ reconciled the whole world to Himself, freely, completely, and fully on the cross. **"[Christ] is the atoning sacrifice for our sins, and not only for ours but also for the sins of the whole world"** (1 John 2:2 NIV).

However, Christianity is also *exclusive:* **"Whoever believes and is baptized will be saved, but *whoever does not believe will be***

condemned" (Mark 16:16, emphasis added). Faith matters. Unbelief kills. Whether it's popular or not, just tell the truth and let God's Word do its thing.

Q: How do you explain the realities of heaven and hell to someone who doesn't believe in God?

A: Thanks to the conscience that God placed in each and every human being, people pretty much get the concept already, even if they don't go to church or read the Bible. Even unbelievers know the basics of right and wrong, know guilt, know spiritual fear, and know deep down inside that they are accountable for the way they live their lives.

Even nonchurchgoers and non-Bible readers know about hell from popular culture. The word *hell* is still the gold standard for the absolute worst possible place and worst possible experience. At every funeral that people attend, they will hear happy talk from the "minister" or whomever about the next life. The word *heavenly* is the gold standard for the very best experience.

What popular culture and our consciences cannot tell us is how to avoid hell and gain heaven. That's where you come in. Only the Bible provides that information. You may be the only Bible reader your unbelieving friend knows. Tell the truth—Jesus said, **"I am the way, and the truth, and the life. No one comes to the Father except through Me"** (John 14:6).

4

"Where two or three are gathered in My name, there am I among them." (Matthew 18:20)

CHURCH LIFE

Q: The Lord's Supper confuses me. How can we receive anything spiritual from a small glass of wine and a little wafer?

A: You can't. The bread and wine aren't the source of Communion's blessings any more than the copper wires in your house are the power to run your furnace or air conditioning. The copper wires are just the conduit, the channel. It's the electrical power humming through those wires that drives the functions of your home. It's not the wires; it's the 200 amps, 100 volts, 60 cycle alternating current that makes everything go.

In the same way, the bread and wine are just the channels God uses to touch you personally. The power comes from the personal promises of Jesus Christ: **"Take, eat; this is *My body*. . . . Drink of it, all of you, for this is *My blood* of the covenant, which is poured out for many for the *forgiveness of sins*"** (Matthew 26:26–28, emphasis added). The real power in the Supper is the Word.

Q: Sometimes you talk about the Sacrament of Baptism or the Sacrament of Communion. What is a sacrament?

A: Alas, this is one of the theological questions about which Christians have not been able to agree. Some say there are seven sacraments, some two, and some say there are none.

I guess it depends on how you define *sacrament*. The word does not exist in the Bible, but like the helpful term *Trinity*, it was coined by Christian teachers long ago to provide a handle for some important biblical concepts. The word is based on the Latin adjective *sacer*, which means "holy." A *sacramentum* is a holy ceremony that

- is instituted by Christ Himself;
- brings Gospel forgiveness to sinful people; and
- connects the powerful Word of God with something tangible, with a physical element, in order to connect the Gospel's blessings physically with an individual.

The only New Testament ceremonies that fit this definition are Baptism and the Lord's Supper. Baptism was instituted by Christ (Matthew 28:18–20), objectively promises forgiveness of sins (Galatians 3:27), and uses an earthly element, water (Ephesians 5:26).

Holy Communion was instituted by Christ (Matthew 26:26–29), promises forgiveness (Matthew 26:28), and uses physical elements to touch individual believers (the bread and wine).

It may seem as though these two sacramental ceremonies do exactly the same thing as proclaiming the saving Word of God. Correct. They do. God has three ways to create and sustain faith in people. Each one in a different way communicates the same objective reality that God loves and forgives us unconditionally. The water, bread, wine, and the pastor don't bring that saving grace. The power behind the Sacraments is God's Word.

The benefit of not only hearing the Good News but also experiencing its personal touch is that you cannot possibly mistake for whom this gift of forgiveness is intended. You could possibly hear the Gospel in a sermon and conclude its pardon is meant for other "good" people. You cannot mistake who is meant when the water of spiritual renewal is splashed on an individual. You might read the Bible and assume that its good news is for others worthier than you, but you cannot mistake whom God loves and forgives when the very body and blood of the Savior are placed right into your mouth.

Q: Why is there so much controversy around women clergy in the church? I don't see the problem with it.

A: The reason for the controversy is that there are some denominations and theologians who do not believe that God provided 100 percent of the content for the Bible. They believe that St. Paul and the other early writers were acting on their own and inserted their own (sometimes chauvinistic) personal opinions into the story. Hence any instructions Paul gave on gender roles could be viewed as obsolete.

Others (including me) believe that every word of the Bible was supervised and ultimately provided by God Himself and that every word therefore bears His authority, clarity, power, and truth. Here is what the Bible says about gender in God's world: Men and women are both created in the image of God, both redeemed equally by the blood of Christ, both loved and valued equally, both gifted for service, and both commissioned to be witnesses for Christ and servants in His name (Acts 2:17–18).

However, in Christian homes and in Christian churches, there are gender distinctions designed by God. Within marriage, God calls the husband the head and the wife a helper suitable for him. Within the Church, **"The head of every man is Christ, and the head of the woman is man"** (1 Corinthians 11:3 NIV). Both 1 Timothy 2:11–12 and 1 Corinthians 14:33–34 challenge men to step up and accept responsibility for their congregations, and these verses direct women to respect that authority, **"as in all the churches of the saints"** (1 Corinthians 14:33).

Q: Sometimes in church I hear our pastor say, "I forgive you all your sins." How is that possible? I thought only God can forgive sins.

A: A crowd that once watched Jesus heal a paralyzed man agreed with you: **"Who can forgive sins but God alone?"** (Mark 2:7). How true. Only the blood of Jesus, paid on the cross and poured out for the world, can remove our sinful guilt in God's court.

However, God empowers all of His Christian believers to be brokers and sharers of the message of that forgiving grace. Every Christian is a royal priest, authorized to assure repentant and fearful sinners that their sins are forgiven (1 Peter 2:9). Jesus told His disciples after His resurrection, **"If you forgive the sins of any, they are forgiven them; if you withhold forgiveness from any, it is withheld"** (John 20:23). The point of Jesus' instruction was not to send a select few on a power trip; it was to encourage people to repent and to encourage people to share Gospel comfort with one another. In your day-to-day life, you and other Christians can participate in the little drama of confession and absolution.

In the church setting, the congregation has called and empowered their pastor to speak to them on God's behalf. There is nothing the pastor has done to merit that forgiveness. He is simply given the privilege to speak Jesus' words to everybody in the room.

Q: When the offering plate goes by me at church, I feel pressure to give. My conscience bothers me, but I'm having a hard time making ends meet as it is. What does the Bible say about how much we should give?

A: Giving offerings to a Christian ministry is not a law; it is a joyful response to the Gospel. In Old Testament times, the tithe (10 percent) was mandatory. In New Testament times, you are invited only to give gifts **"in keeping with [your] income"** (1 Corinthians 16:2 NIV). Your gift-giving decisions are between you and God, and they are an important part of your worship life.

God does not expect you to give something you do not have. The gifts that we do give came from Him in the first place. We are only returning to Him what was originally His. Giving is for everybody, not just the wealthy (**"on the first day of every week, *each one of you should set aside a sum of money in keeping with his income*"** 1 Corinthians 16:12 NIV, emphasis added). I enjoy watching our grade school children come to the altar with their pennies. It is not the quantity of money in the exchange that matters, but joy and worship in the heart. The highest praise that Jesus ever gave was to a widow who contributed two *lepta* (literally her two cents' worth) to the temple ministries (Mark 12:42). It was all the money she had that day and probably meant she went hungry. Her desire to worship was even greater than her hunger.

The main reason for giving is not the institutional demands of running the business of a congregation. We don't pass the plate so we can pay the light bill. The main reason for giving is to provide an opportunity for worship.

Here are some of my thoughts about money:

- Spend less than your income.

- Worship God with joy and gratitude when you give.

- Trust and expect that God will not allow you to suffer because of your generosity but will instead more than compensate you. God's promise: "You will be enriched in every way to be generous in every way" (2 Corinthians 9:11).

Q: Should any church that uses *Christian* in its name be considered okay to follow? Will it get me through that narrow door to heaven and profess the one true faith? We have a lot of "feel -good" churches around that sound all well and good, but something's missing—something important. Still, whatever it is, these congregations are leading families to their pews.

A: Alas, names don't mean much, at least on the surface. Any religious organization may call itself anything it wants to, but some of these groups want to define for themselves what those names mean. You cannot assume that every religious organization means the same things when using a term or name.

A nonnegotiable core principle to me is whether or not a congregation or church organization accepts the Bible as the inerrant and infallible source of information and authority for all teaching. If the Bible does not have final and supreme authority, man-made and often erroneous notions creep in. Denominational traditions and church politics can take the place of revealed truth.

Any congregation or church body worth a dime will have a written statement of beliefs. Those should be examined carefully and compared with the Bible's teachings. Go slow in committing. Talk with a pastor you trust about evaluating new congregations.

I'm not completely sure what you mean by "feel-good" churches. It appears that you mean it as a criticism. Indeed, if a congregation cares only about feelings and emotions and doesn't have solid biblical content, you need to steer clear. On the other hand, what is the opposite of a "feel-good" church? A "feel-miserable" church? Do you want to be part of a group with that descriptor?

A healthy congregation has serious Bible study, joyful worship, and loving relationships. Your brain will be fed and your soul will be nourished, and your heart will feel good as you drive home.

Q: My father taught us that you should choose a church by the Word spoken there, not by the pastor or the people in attendance. Can you share any additional words of wisdom on that topic?

A: A similar question to the preceding. When you are looking for a local congregation to attend and then join, my first piece of advice is not to be in a hurry. It's impossible to grasp in just one or two Sunday visits what the organization really stands for.

My second piece of advice is to visit around and to get around so you know what your choices are. The Internet is a fabulous help for that activity.

My third piece of advice is that you cannot always assume that a denominational tag will necessarily represent everything that people have historically understood by that denomination. Sometimes there are movements within denominations that believe quite differently from what other congregations with that same name might believe.

Here are the things that I think are what you want to look for. Number one: first and foremost, does this organization grasp the inerrant, infallible, inspired, and authoritative Word of God and place it at the center of all its beliefs? Is the Word of God at the core of all messages that you will be hearing? Will its leaders tell you that they believe in Scripture's inerrancy, meaning there are no errors, false teachings, or human mistakes in the Bible?

Are the sacraments there? God gave us Baptism and Holy Communion as additional means with which to touch an individual with the Gospel and to build up our faith and confidence in the forgiveness of our sins. Does the organization believe in the power of Baptism, and does it believe in the reality of the body and blood of Christ being given to people for the forgiveness of their sins?

Should the pastor or people be irrelevant—only focusing on the message? Well, I would look for what kind of communication is happening. The main speaker is the person from whom you will need to be drawing your food. If it's someone you can't bear to listen to or someone who's not speaking to your heart, my advice is that your search is not done yet.

You need to be in a position where you want to go to church, not "Oh, it's Sunday, so I have to go. I don't get anything out of the messages, but I should go there because of some sort of obligation." If that's where you are, you're not going to last. Without joy in your heart, you will find yourself rebelling against it and hating the experience. In my humble opinion, I really do think the messenger has a part to play in this decision. That person will be your safari guide on your adventures in the Word, and you have to trust him and be willing to open your heart to his guidance.

Lastly, I really do think the people matter. If they're cold to you, if nobody pays any attention to you, there's something missing from the love dynamic that needs to be going on in a healthy congregation. A place that is full of people who are into their own agendas and who pay no attention to you is going to make it very hard for you to get involved and become an active worker and volunteer and servant in that organization.

On the other hand, if there's a living and vital faith in the place, you will be able to perceive it and feel it.

Q: What's the proper worship style for a church to have in its worship services?

A: I guess the best answer that I can give you is that the Lord has given every Christian congregation a great deal of freedom in the ways in which it carries out its worship. Every group has the God-given right to set up worship styles and practices that the members think will be most effective in carrying out its Gospel mission in its community.

Some congregations are very "high church." They use robes, candles, chanting, a lot of symbolic gestures, and traditions. On the other hand, some congregations are very "low church." Perhaps their pastors don't wear robes at all but instead wear street clothes with no jackets or ties. Or even jeans! They want to create an environment where people can dress casually, where they can come and still feel welcome and accepted. They want to provide an alternative space for people who are turned off by "churchiness."

Strong and persuasive arguments can be made for both styles. Every congregation has to work out its own way to do what it thinks will best connect with its membership. What really matters is not so much the outward appearances. What matters is the message. Is the Word explained? Is the Gospel proclaimed? Are the Sacraments administered? Do people worship from the heart and head? Will they experience Bible studying, singing, praying, giving, serving, and fellowship?

Q: Sometimes you encourage viewers to go to church along with watching *Time of Grace*. What's wrong with using *Time of Grace* as my only worship opportunity? I don't really think I need to go to an actual church since I'm getting an excellent message every week from you right in my home.

A: I have good news and bad news. The good news is that I'm thrilled that you find value in the programs. Through the miracle of mass media, you and I can go on a personal adventure each week into God's wonderful Word.

The bad news is that you deprive yourself of important gifts from God if you stay at a distance from a congregation. You will miss the thrill of receiving Christ's body and blood in the Lord's Supper—God's most intimate and personal touch in our lives. You will miss out on warm and supportive fellowship of people whom God could send into your life to give you encouragement when you're down, correction when you're on a bad path, and comfort when you're grieving.

You will also miss out on opportunities to find your own personal ministry of faith service as you use the gifts God has given you. You will miss the thrill of worship with other Christians, singing and praying and praising the Savior who gave you new life. Of the many more reasons I could list, let one last compelling reason be mentioned: you will miss the joy of being part of outreach and mission work, spreading the Gospel with other Christians to people who haven't heard it yet.

Q: What is the difference between passive and active faith?

A: I think when people use those terms, they are trying to draw a distinction between people who live out their faith (i.e., attend worship, read the Bible, pray, witness, give offerings, volunteer) as opposed to those who believe in their hearts but don't act visibly on their beliefs.

To me it's a dangerous distinction. The Bible doesn't describe two kinds of faith. There is only one kind of faith. True faith of the mind and heart automatically brings forth fruits of faith (read Galatians 5 and James 2). James uses a hard term for fruitless faith— he calls it *dead* faith.

Are you actively seeking to live out your faith? Let's pay attention to the so-called passive believers among us and draw them lovingly into the warm worship and fellowship life of the Church. Let's never settle for a faith that is inactive, either in ourselves or people we know.

Q: God wants us to obey the Ten Commandments, of which one is to keep the Sabbath Day holy. I'm confused regarding what God means by the Sabbath Day. Sunday is a traditional church day, but God rested on the seventh day of creation. Which day is the correct Sabbath Day, and is that the only true worship day?

A: The answer to that question depends on which century you are living in. If you were an Israelite from the year 1400 BC until the time of Christ, you lived under the old covenant. There was to be no work on Saturday, the seventh day, and all household and farm chores were to be kept to an absolute minimum. Saturday was synagogue day. The Third Commandment, "Remember the Sabbath Day by keeping it holy," uses old covenant language.

But you are reading this right now, so that means you are living in the twenty-first century. You now live under the new covenant, which has replaced the old. Colossians 2:16–17 removes the work prohibition from Saturday and, in fact, allows us to use our judgment as to our weekly worship and religious festivals as well.

Some Christians, earnestly trying to help people get a regular worship life, have taught that Sunday is the new Sabbath Day. There are still towns and entire counties with "blue laws," which forbid the sale of alcohol on Sunday, for instance. But Sunday is not the Sabbath Day. The earliest Christians worshiped on Saturday, the original Sabbath Day, but then of their own free choice moved to Sunday as a worship day to commemorate the beginning of creation, Jesus' grand resurrection, and the coming of the Holy Spirit on Pentecost. Numerous congregations these days offer worship services on all the other six days of the week as well. It is their privilege. God loves Tuesday worship as much as Sunday worship.

Hebrews 4 teaches how Christians today keep the Third Commandment and honor God's Sabbath. The true Sabbath is God's gift to us of the forgiveness of our sins through Jesus, not the setting apart of any particular day of the week. That's the true rest that Jesus promises in Matthew 11:28–30: rest for your soul.

Q: Why does the date of Easter bounce around each year?

A: It's because the early Christians wanted to celebrate the resurrection right around the time of the Jewish Passover (just as

Jesus ate the Passover meal with His disciples on Maundy Thursday evening). The Jewish rabbis would set the date for Passover on the basis of Leviticus 23:5: **"In the first month, on the fourteenth day of the month at twilight, is the Lord's Passover"** (not our January, but the month of Nisan in the Jewish calendar). The ancient Hebrew calendar was based on lunar months and does not coincide with our Roman-based solar calendar. Hence, Passover lands on different chronological dates each year.

The Council of Nicaea was called in AD 325 to resolve doctrinal problems about the identity of Jesus Christ. That's where the main part of our Nicene Creed comes from. But believe it or not, the second most urgent item on the agenda was agreeing on a common date for Easter. After lengthy debate, the decision was made to set the date on the Sunday following the fourteenth day of the paschal moon (i.e., the first full moon on or following the vernal equinox, March 21). That's why today we have a range from March 22 to April 25 when Easter Sunday can occur.

Q: Some people say that Easter has pagan origins. Is that true?

A: Well, sort of. The concept of celebrating the resurrection of Jesus is purely scriptural, of course. In some languages, the name for the celebration comes from the Hebrew word for Passover, *Pesach*. The Greek word for Passover, for instance, is *Pascha* (from which we get our word *paschal* in reference to certain liturgical candles and the Lamb). The traditional Easter Epistle, 1 Corinthians 5:7, says, **"Christ, our Passover lamb, has been sacrificed."** The French word *Pâques* and Spanish word *Pascuas* name Easter by its connection to the Passover.

This is not in English or German. The English historian Bede (AD 673–735) says that the word *Easter* (in German *Ostern)* comes from the Germanic pagan deity *Ēostre*, goddess of the dawn and of springtime. Just as early Christians arbitrarily chose a date for the birthday of Christ that roughly coincided with the pagan Roman feast of Saturnalia around the winter solstice, so the Germanic/Anglo-Saxon Christians probably chose the word *Easter* to ease the transition of pagans into the Christian Church.

Just as there is secular Christmas with Santa and reindeer myths, there are still remnants of Ēostre worship in the rabbits, eggs, and nests (baskets with green plastic grass) that are used in the United States today. We can thank German immigrants for that. Rabbits and eggs are ancient symbols of fertility, a concept very much on the minds of farm folk as spring is beginning.

Whether or not you eat hard-boiled eggs, chocolate bunnies, and ham on the big day is up to you. What is not negotiable, however, is to give Jesus Christ worship, honor, and praise from the bottom of our hearts and top of our lungs for His mighty victory over sin, death, and Satan. The Lord is risen! He is risen indeed!

Q: Can you explain what it means when you say there is power in Baptism? Does it mean that I'm saved if I am baptized?

A: You have put your finger squarely on one of the sorest points of contention in all Christian history. For many centuries, Christians have been sadly divided on what Baptism is and what it does for people.

Your questions are closely related but not quite identical. Baptism does indeed have power. It is not merely a human ceremony or declarative act by an individual, but it is a mighty outpouring of the Holy Spirit. Paul wrote in Titus 3:5, **"[God] saved us . . . by the washing of regeneration and renewal of the Holy Spirit."** In Ephesians 5:26, he says that Christ cleanses the Church **"by the washing of water through the word."** In Galatians 3:27, he says that in Baptism we **"put on Christ"** (i.e., wear His holiness).

When you were baptized, you inherited spiritual wealth that was bought for you by Christ on His cross. Baptism has no meaning apart from the cross. The Word of God spoken along with the water is a power source that brings the Gospel message from God to you: "I love you. I forgive you." **"Whoever believes and is baptized will be saved"** (Mark 16:16). **"Baptism, which corresponds to this** [i.e., the flood], **now saves you, not as a removal of dirt from the body but as an appeal to God for a good conscience, through the resurrection of Jesus Christ"** (1 Peter 3:21).

Baptism doesn't make hearing and learning the Word of God unnecessary or irrelevant. Growth in the Word is vital to our spiritual health, since Satan will attack us relentlessly to try to cause us to fall away.

Q: The words *Trinity* and *triune* are not used in the Bible. How then can the teaching of the Trinity be considered biblical?

A: A most appropriate caution—to be very, very careful in Christian terminology and doctrinal statements so we don't introduce our own conclusions, notions, and opinions into God's wonderful truth. It is best to try to use exact words from the Bible whenever we can in organizing our summaries of the Bible's teachings.

Still, some words coined by Christian teachers long ago have proven helpful in communicating the truths of the Bible. Terms such as *sacrament, six-day creation, inerrancy,* and *verbal inspiration* help us sum up and remember what God has said and done.

The words *triune* and *Trinity* come from the two Latin words for "one" and "three." They summarize the staggering mystery that our God is one essence and three persons at the same time. See Deuteronomy 6:4 for the "oneness" and Matthew 28:19–20 for the "threeness."

Thus, the words *triune* and *Trinity* do not come from the Bible, but the concepts they summarize do.

Q: Do you have any comments or thoughts on the Lake of Fire and Book of Life in Revelation? Those things are a very integral part of the church my children belong to, and this is troubling to me.

A: Those phrases appear at the end of Revelation 20. The lake of fire, also called the second death, is a metaphor for final judgment, condemnation, and everlasting destruction. It is a terrifying picture that God will hold accountable every man, woman, and demon who rebelled against Him. Their fate will be horrible, and it will never end. Satan himself will end up there.

The Book of Life is a metaphor for the registry of all believers. Your name was written there from all eternity when God chose you; it glowed with life when you became a believer through water and the Word, and your heart will throb with joy when you "see" it written there when you come home to heaven. Jesus teaches that He is the Bread of Life; whoever eats that food (i.e., believes in Him) will have eternal life. All believers in Jesus have their names written in His book.

Q: Can you explain the purpose of having both Law and Gospel in a church service?

A: Law and Gospel are essential not only for church services but also for all summaries of God's teachings. They are the two principal messages that the Bible communicates to humankind. They are two things you must know before the final exam.

Romans 3:23–25 has an elegant summary of each: **"All have sinned and fall short of the glory of God"** (vv. 2–3) articulates the dilemma into which each of us was born. We inherited Adam and Eve's sinful disease and then added our own evil actions. We are incapable of saving ourselves, getting rid of our guilt, escaping hell, and reconnecting with God.

The Gospel brings us news of what a loving God did about our predicament: we **"are justified by His grace as a gift, through the redemption that is in Christ Jesus, whom God put forward as a propitiation by His blood, to be received by faith"** (vv. 24–25) It is my hope that every Christian church on the face of the earth sends its worshipers home with that certainty in each heart. Fear and weakness and doubt gnaw away at that confidence each day, and we need to be refueled with Gospel power through Word and Sacrament.

This is the great story of the Bible and deserves to be expressed in our liturgies, prayers, songs, and sermons.

Q: Do I need to be concerned about the difference between venial and mortal sins? Isn't a sin a sin?

A: Sin is indeed a sin. You will not find a distinction between mortal and venial sins in the Bible. These terms are unique to the Catholic Church and go back at least to the teachings of Thomas Aquinas in the 1200s. Some trace the concepts clear back to Augustine in the 400s. But they aren't in the Bible—they come from Catholic moral philosophy. The idea is that some sins, while bad, won't put you in hell, and others are so grave that you incur damnation.

In my view, the distinction is not only unbiblical, it is not helpful either. Every thought, word, and deed in our lives that disobeys God is evil, flowing from the inborn rebelliousness that we inherited from our parents. Our real problem is not these or those sins, but sin itself. No sin is so small that it doesn't matter; no sin is so great that Christ's blood atonement is not greater still.

Stand with me at the foot of the cross and hear Jesus' words of hope offered to a violent criminal, rightly being executed as a menace to society: "**'Jesus, remember me when You come into Your kingdom.' And [Jesus] said to him, 'Truly, I say to you, today you will be with Me in Paradise'**" (Luke 23:42–43).

Q: What if I don't have any special gifts or talents? How can I serve God and others in my church family?

A: You are off the rails with your first statement. There are certain high-profile gifts in the Church that people see right away— the gift to play the piano or organ proficiently, the gifts of vocal artistry, administration, or public speaking. But families and congregations are held together and blessed by many, many more wonderful talents and servant-gifts, often utilized quietly or behind the scenes, which don't get noticed as often but are still vital. Romans 12:5–8 mentions some valuable heaven-sent gifts: serving, teaching, encouraging, contributing, leading, showing mercy.

Self-awareness can take years to develop, and often we aren't sure who we are or what we're good at or good for. When you are puzzled about your own gifts—and you do have them—ask two things. First, what do others say about me? You might be surprised at the value that others perceive that you bring to the group. Second, what am I passionate about? Where do you have a burn? Where can you spend hours that fly by like minutes because you love the work?

Here are gifts that I have noticed in my ministry and for which I am grateful to God and appreciative of the gifted servants He sent us: people who have the patience and skill to care for and teach little children; people who have a passion for preparing and serving good food; people who are organized and can organize others; people who like to see little columns of numbers add up and who can budget and reconcile bank statements; people who have a green thumb; people with compassionate hearts who care about finding the lost, reassuring the fearful, crying with the grieving, and hugging those who feel that they have no friends.

Q: In the Lord's Prayer, we pray, "Forgive us our trespasses as we forgive those who trespass against us." I was told once as a child that if I don't forgive others, God won't forgive me. That was terrifying to me. I now know that we forgive because God forgives us. Why the misleading wording?

A: Well, we do indeed forgive others because God forgives us. The Gospel drives all of our Christian behaviors. But you weren't exactly lied to. In the middle of the Sermon on the Mount

(Matthew 5–7), Jesus set forth His magnificent prayer, which we now call "The Lord's." But then He added this grave warning, **"If you forgive men when they sin against you, your heavenly Father will also forgive you. But if you do not forgive men their sins, your Father will not forgive your sins"** (Matthew 6:14–5).

For an expanded treatment of the same subject, read Jesus' marvelous parable of the unmerciful servant, found in Matthew 18:21–35 and note its solemn conclusion: **"This is how My heavenly Father will treat each of you unless you forgive your brother from your heart"** (v. 35 NIV).

Here is a good example of the two main teachings of the Bible, the Law and the Gospel. The Law expresses God's holy and pure demands; the Gospel brings poor, guilty sinners the free forgiveness of Christ. The Law threatens; the Gospel assures.

Here's our solace: as long as we believe in Christ as our Savior, we live and breathe under the Gospel. We are spared the condemnations of the Law. But now we come full circle—that pardon doesn't allow us to go back and live like heathens again. The relief and hope in our hearts lead us in gratitude to want to serve God, and one way we can do that is by showing the other sinners around us the same mercy that God has shown us. May you find joy in forgiving those who trespass against you!

5

"Whether you eat or drink, or whatever
you do, do all to the glory of God."

(1 Corinthians 10:31)

LIVING FOR GOD

Q: Satan is a tempter, no doubt. He leads us astray constantly. But can he really put thoughts into our heads? What is the devil's status in this world? Does he really have power over us?

A: God's archenemy hates you. He seeks to destroy you in body, mind, and spirit. He seeks to tempt and seduce and lie to and betray the believers to drag them back to their original lost state: **"You were dead in the trespasses and sins in which you once walked, following the course of this world, following the prince of the power of the air, the spirit that is now at work in the sons of disobedience"** (Ephesians 2:1–2).

Isn't that a scary revelation about the devil? That he glides around through the air and does his dirty work from within people? How can we be protected from this hideous force?

Christ's victory on the cross and His resurrection from the tomb have dealt Satan a mortal wound, though he is still afoot and dangerous. But the believers triumph with Christ as long as they are connected to Him by faith and holding fast to the Word. **"They have conquered [Satan] by the blood of the Lamb and by the word of** their testimony" (Revelation 12:11). He cannot win: **"The God of peace will soon crush Satan under your feet"** (Romans 16:20).

Q: In the psalms, King David often asks God to destroy or kill his enemies in various ways, and he shows hatred for them. Yet we are told that we must completely forgive our enemies. What am I missing?

A: You aren't missing anything—it's a great question. These psalm verses, called the "imprecatory" psalms (i.e., the psalms that call down curses), do seem to violate Christ's maxim about turning the other cheek, don't they? But these psalms are part of God's revealed Word and carry His divine intent and authority. Why would God permit, or even instruct, His people to say such things?

1. King David, writer of many of these "curses," was legendary for never taking personal vengeance. Read how he spared his enemies to wait for the Lord in 1 Samuel 24 and 26 and in 2 Samuel 16, 18, and 19. Although attacked by Saul, Shimei, and Absalom his own son, David bore his sufferings bravely and let God take care of the revenge. David was no vigilante, no Rambo or Dirty Harry. He believed, and we should too, that **"vengeance is Mine, I will repay, says the Lord"** (Romans 12:19).

2. Christ Jesus did indeed teach patience and self-control with His counsel about cheek turning. He also pronounced His own string of curses on those who opposed and tried to sabotage God's plans (read Matthew 23). The enemies that David prayed against weren't his personal foes only; they were enemies of God who were seeking to destroy God's Church. Their destruction would bring peace and safety to suffering

believers, and David prayed for that to happen to spare the lives and souls of the believers.

Q: I'm eighty-four and the Bible only takes us up to seventy. Your magazine has had articles such as "Can't Wait to Get to Heaven" and "Jesus, Get Me out of Here." It seems like we need a message on growing old and waiting for the end. What should we do with ourselves while we wait?

A: Your letter embarrasses me. It makes me aware that I don't know if I have been a very good teacher in articulating the great value that God's seniors have and the value they bring to their families, their communities, and especially to their congregations. God's seniors aren't just killing time waiting for the angels; they are important members of the team.

The writer says, "I'm eighty-four but the Bible only takes us up to seventy." I think she's referring to words of Moses in Psalm 90:10. Moses writes, **"The years of our life are seventy, or even by reason of strength eighty; yet their span is but toil and trouble; they are soon gone, and we fly away."**

Does that psalm make it look like you might have a decent life until you're seventy, or maybe eighty if you're lucky, and then that's about the end of it? What if you're older than eighty—is there a use for you, or are you just waiting for the bus?

"What should we do with ourselves?" is a question that haunts me. I am grateful to have the opportunity in this book to express my admiration and appreciation for the value that God's seniors bring. They call you "octogenarians." That doesn't mean that you're washed up! Did you know that Moses himself began his leadership of the people of Israel when he was eighty? God didn't think he was mature enough for that big job until he was an octogenarian.

Abraham, the father of all believers, did not become a father until he was in his nineties. Sarah conceived Isaac, the miracle child, when she was eighty-nine. The prophetess Anna was eighty-four when she met Jesus and honored Him with a special prophetic utterance (Luke 2:36–38). St. John wrote his Gospel, his three letters, and the astonishing visions of Revelation when he was in his nineties.

People who are full of years have all kinds of things that they can do for the younger generation. For one, they can tell the stories of where the family came from. Every time an older person dies, it's like a neighborhood library burns down. Tell the stories; write them down or dictate them into a recorder. You can collect all your family pictures and make sure they don't get lost or damaged. Since you may be the only one left who knows who all those people are, you can label the pictures so your family and descendants know at whom they're looking.

In my home, four of my most precious possessions are shoe boxes full of old family photos, some of them going back into the 1800s. I would have no idea who those people were if relatives of mine, older than I, had not carefully written down who those people were. I am grateful.

In your retirement years, you finally have time to pray. Actually, we all have time to pray, but in our middle years we don't think we do because we're so busy trying to earn a living, taking care of our family and kids, and managing the house. We forget, and sometimes days, maybe weeks, slide by without any serious time for reflection and prayer. When you are retired, God gives you that gift of time. You can pray for those whom you love, you can pray for your pastor, you can pray for your church (and you might even be able to squeeze in time to pray for me).

Your congregation has all kinds of work that needs to be done during the day when the middle generation is at work. When my travels have me visiting churches during the week, I love seeing the seniors on campus working on projects or helping people.

Q: How do angels help us? Do they keep us from sinning?

A: Next to God Himself, angels are your best friends. They are God's agents to carry out His mission to bring all believers home safely to heaven. They are **"ministering spirits sent out to serve for the sake of those who are to inherit salvation"** (Hebrews 1:14).

The Bible tells us that angels provide protection to believers from Satan, his demons, and Satan's human agents of evil. They protect believers from accidental harm (Psalm 91). They provide information and guidance to believers and help them in their time of need. Angels will round up unbelievers on the Day of Judgment as God's imperial bailiffs, but they will also serve as your personal escorts and rides as you watch God re-create a new heaven and new earth.

Children especially benefit from angel service; Jesus told His disciples, **"See that you do not despise one of these little ones. For I tell you that in heaven their angels always see the face of My Father who is in heaven"** (Matthew 18:10). But I know of no Scripture passage that promises that angels will be sent to keep us from sinning.

Q: Do I have to pray in a special way in order for God to hear me?

A: No.

Just talk to Him. You can murmur, cry out, whisper, sing, or just think your prayer thoughts. You can pray standing, sitting, kneeling, running, driving in your car, or lying down. Morning, afternoon, evening, and the middle of the night are all fine times to pray—He's open twenty-four hours, weekends included. Weekends especially. Pray alone or with a friend or with your family or with friends or at work or in a Bible study or in church. But do pray, trusting in Jesus as your Savior—He alone is the way to the Father's throne.

Q: I have a decision to make. How do I know I'm making the right one?

A: We all yearn for signs from God so that we know which of the choices before us is the best. God chose to give personal signs in a few exceptional cases in Bible times (such as Gideon's fleece), but most of the time, He wants believers to use their common sense and what they know of His principles to make choices in life.

Sometimes we don't have a right or wrong choice—God would be happy with any number of outcomes. God chooses not to intervene directly in our lives to instruct us whom to date, whom to marry, to which companies to send our resumes, which people to interview or hire, which car to buy, where to live, or what color to paint our houses. He loves it when we grow in our ability to show spiritual discernment and make wise moves.

His Word contains powerful general principles, and He wants us to know them and use them. He wants us to know His Ten Commandments, for instance, which are a very handy summary of His will for all humankind. Do you know where they are in the Bible?

Do you know where to look for dating guidance, principles for a happy marriage, advice on parenting, and work attitudes?

One often overlooked book of the Bible for growth in developing a personal value system based on God's wisdom is the Book of Proverbs. In fact, may I suggest that you put this book down and read a chapter of Proverbs right now?

Q: I've done a lot of bad things in my life—many things I'm ashamed of and feel very guilty about. The Bible says that Jesus took my sins away, but is it really true?

A: Your question is central to your existence and to the lives and eternity of everybody in the history of this planet. It is the most important question in the world. Here is what you need to know from sacred Scripture:

1. Everybody sins. Everybody is born with rebellion sickness. You are indeed a bad person, but so is everybody else, me included. When you read the stories of the greatest heroes in the Bible, you will discover that they were also liars, thieves, adulterers, murderers, swindlers, and terrible parents.

2. Everybody is loved by Jesus Christ the Savior. God the Father loved the world (a world full of sinners) so much that He sent His one and only Son to suffer and die in our place. He took our blame, bore our sentence, absorbed our punishment in His body, and thus paid all our debts. Yours included. The small debts, medium debts, and the big ugly debts. All paid in full.

3. Everyone who believes that point two, above, is true receives full forgiveness of all debts, judgments, and punishments.

4. Now get into your Bible and find out the kinds of behaviors that God loves. Powered by the Holy Spirit, who now lives within you, you can be so useful to God. In fact, some of God's greatest servants are driven by their immense gratitude for being loved and saved. Read the story of the anointing of Jesus by a sinful woman, Luke 7:36–50. She loved much because she had been forgiven much.

Q: How does free will fit into God's plans for our lives? If God has my life all mapped out, do I really have free will?

A: Your question has vexed Christians small and great, old and young, PhDs and children, for many centuries. Untangling the interplay between God's choices and our choices, God's will and our will, God's actions and our actions, His causing and our causing, is probably beyond anyone but God Himself.

Here are a few principles from Scripture to create a little less mess in your mind (we won't get it all until we're in heaven):

- You are spiritually dead at birth (Ephesians 2:1–3). Although you can make decisions about which clothes to wear and which career to pursue, you aren't in tune with God and desire the opposite of His will. **"The mind that is set on the flesh is hostile to God, for it does not submit to God's law; indeed, it cannot. Those who are in the flesh cannot please God"** (Romans 8:6–8).

- You became a believer by the eternal choice of God (Ephesians 1:3–14), by the universal atonement of Christ (2 Corinthians 5:19), by the powerful working of the Holy Spirit (1 Corinthians 12:3), through the power of Word and

Sacrament (Ephesians 5:26). It was not you who found God; it was He who found you and changed you.

- Your will is now reborn. Your dead heart is now alive. Your corrupted will is now capable of making godly choices. You can indeed do all things through Him who gives you strength (Philippians 4:13). But while we live in this world, on this earth, the sinful nature we inherited persists. We have been made holy by Christ, but our will is not perfected until we are in heaven.

- The fact that God knows what is going to happen does not mean that He has caused everything to happen. This is a great mystery, born of the limitations of our inherited sinful nature, to grasp how we, who live in the moving snapshot of the present, interact with God, who knows no limits of time. Here is the riddle—although God knows all of human experience at a glance, although He simultaneously lives in past, present, and future, He chooses to interact with us through His love. We still make bad choices, but God's choice to love us through Christ sanctifies us. In other words, our choices and actions *really do matter.*

In short, does God know everything that will happen to us? Is everything under His guidance and control? Do believers have free will? Yes to all three.

Q: Something that is not brought up very often from the pulpit is the concept of love. I think it's important. When I send out letters to people, I always sign them, "Sent with my love." Is there any Scripture that tells us about demonstrating love?

A: Loving others and being loved is a big deal. I have two suggestions for you. One is that you read the entire Epistle of 1 John. Writing as an old man, John concentrates on just a very few things, the main one being his passionate exhortations to love and take care of other people. Take note of how much of 1 John is devoted to encouraging his readers to love one another.

My second suggestion is to study John 13. John was present in the upper room on Maundy Thursday evening when Jesus said, **"A new commandment I give to you, that you love one another"** (v. 34). Now, it's not as though God invented love on Maundy Thursday evening, but the new covenant that Jesus brought about, what you might call the New Testament era in which we live, *must* have love as its trademark or characteristic.

"Love one another: just as I have loved you, you also are to love one another. By this all people will know that you are My disciples, if you have love for one another" (vv. 34–35). The new covenant—that is, the basis for God's relationship with us in the New Testament times in which we live—is based on Jesus' love for us. How could He love you more than by coming from His comfortable world in heaven and stooping to live here, emptied of all His glory, treated like a servant? He came to be a slave. He spent Himself teaching and healing people. He ended up being crucified for us, willing to do that because that's how much He wants you to live with Him forever. How could that be anything other than pure love?

Now the point—Jesus invites us all to treat the other people in our lives the same way that He has treated us: with *patience*, knowing one another's weaknesses; with *kindness*, treating one another better than they deserve; with *gentleness*, instead of abuse or criticism, building people up and encouraging them; with *compassion*, that is, being willing to share their pain and carry some of their load; and with *forgiveness*, letting our debtors off the hook just as we were freely forgiven by Christ.

✳✳

Q: What's the main thing God expects of us? What is His primary goal for us?

A: I will let Jesus Himself answer your question. People asked Him once, **" 'What must we do, to be doing the works of God?' Jesus answered them, 'This is the work of God, that you believe in Him whom He has sent' "** (John 6:28–29).

Perhaps that sounds simplistic, but if you are connected in faith to Jesus Christ, everything else will fall into place over time. Connected to Jesus, you will want to hear and read more of the Word of God, the Bible, which will deepen your faith and guide your attitudes and behaviors. You will grow in love and service, becoming more useful to God each day. And you will be judged holy and righteous on the Last Day.

It is the desire of God's heart for you to make it home to heaven. We may be sprinting or crawling, rich or poor, famous or nobodies; we might live in mansions or in little cottages or in tents; but if He gets us to the finish line still believers in Christ, we will live forever with Him in His beautiful new kingdom. It's all ours through faith.

✳✳

Q: Can you tell me how to do a better job of living a Christian life Monday through Saturday?

A: No matter how great your study and worship on Sunday is, that spiritual experience is not enough to sustain your life for six more days. My counsel is that you plan some personal spiritual time each day. If you're a morning person, then do it first thing. If you have a long lunch break, do it in the middle. If you are a night person like me, evenings are best.

Set aside a little piece of time that you will jealously guard, and do two powerful things: let God speak to you through His Word, and then let God hear from you in prayer.

For additional growth and strength,

- keep a prayer journal with dates so you can keep track of your spiritual progress;

- get involved in a small-group Bible study in which you can learn from other Christians and share what you know;

- watch some Christian videos instead of soaps, reality shows, and sports, and get some recommendations for Christian books on topics in which you would like to grow; and

- get involved in a service project in which you serve somebody else.

Q: Does coveting include things like gambling? Is gambling a sin or not?

A: Gambling used to be restricted to places like Las Vegas and Atlantic City, but now it's everywhere. Millions and millions of Americans, Christians included, play the slots, buy lottery tickets, play online poker, and bet on sports games. Although the Bible doesn't use the word *gambling* per se, the concept was very well known throughout Bible times.

It is important that we steer a middle course here. When the Bible neither commands nor forbids some kind of human activity (remember the word *adiaphoron*?), God expects us to use our good judgment. If God has not called it sin in and of itself, we shouldn't either.

But—gambling can easily *become* a sin if:

- you are stealing money from God to gamble. (Have you set aside for God a joyful percentage of your income first? What do your weekly offerings look like?)

- you are stealing from your family. (Are your spouse's and children's needs taken care of?)

- your dreams of quick money make you despise earning money through your job and you come to hate the slow pace of paychecks and saving.

- the people with whom you are gambling can't afford it.

- you want to win so badly that you cheat.

Q: What would you say is our responsibility as Christians when it comes to the topic of abortion? What is God's view on the subject?

A: Abortion supporters base their entire argument on the issue of women's rights: it is the *mother*, they say, who should have total control over deciding if what is in her womb is a person or merely tissue that she can surgically remove if inconvenient to her. God's view is summed up in the matchless words of Psalm 139:13: **"You formed my inward parts; You knitted me together in my mother's womb."** God thinks *He* is the Creator of that tiny life; He thinks *He* has the sovereign power and authority to call the unborn what they really are—people.

Now what? What is our responsibility? Social action is a matter of conscience. Christians have many ways to bring God's message to the world. Here are a few suggestions:

- Contribute funds to pro-life organizations. Many not only discourage abortion, but they also connect a woman who has a problem pregnancy with resources to help her care for the baby or place the child for adoption.

- Speak up when you hear abortion-on-demand advocated. You don't have to argue. Just tell the truth. It's a baby, not a fetus. It's a baby, not the product of conception. It's a baby, not tissue.

- Get into the Word and prepare yourself with the things God has said about human life and His creative activity in the womb. Probably not too many people care about your opinions; everybody's got 'em. However, many care about what God says and wants. Quote Him, not yourself.

- Find ways to volunteer at your local pro-life advocacy organization.

- Let your elected officials and candidates know that their abortion views will influence how you vote.

Q: How does one "feel" God in his or her life?

A: Emotions should never come first, and we should never draw conclusions about God on the basis of how we feel. You may encounter a blue stretch in your life and assume that God has stopped caring about you. Wrong. You may suffer some reverses, and in your pain you may assume that these are punishments from God. Wrong.

What comes first is listening to the Word. There we learn of the greatness of our God. How can you not feel awe at the immense size and complexity and beauty of the universe? There we learn of God incarnate, Jesus Christ made flesh, come to earth to rescue us. There we see His miracles, hear His voice, and behold His ultimate sacrifice. How can you not feel both shame at your sins and also sweet relief of freedom from sin's guilt through His death on Calvary?

Psalm 51:12 helps us pray, **"Restore to me the joy of Your salvation."** If you would like not only to know about but also to experience God's goodness, let His Word reveal God to you and pray that He will lift your spirit.

Q: The Bible says that our bodies are temples of the Holy Spirit. If so, shouldn't we keep them intact without defilement? I'm thinking of tattoos specifically.

A: The Bible does not forbid inking one's skin, and so tattooing is one of those areas that belongs to your own judgment.

Do you see tattooing as a form of skin pollution? Do you see it as body graffiti? Then don't do it.

On the other hand, do you see body art as beautiful? Does it give you a sense of belonging? Does putting an image or word permanently on your body represent a deep form of commitment to someone or something you love passionately? Then have at it. Just remember that tattoos go on easier than they come off, should you change your mind later in life.

What the Holy Spirit is really interested in is not your outsides. If you choose to "improve" your natural looks with hair dyes, highlights, perms, makeup, liposuction, Botox, piercing, or a little nip and tuck here and there, that's your business. What the Spirit is interested in is the content of your character, the beliefs of your soul, and the quality of your behaviors. You worship God best not with your personal appearance, but with words and deeds that come from faith in your Savior, Jesus.

Q: I feel like God has given up on me, and I have a hard time letting go of past hurts and forgiving the wrongdoings of myself and others. I know I've made a lot of wrong choices, a lot of mistakes that now I regret. I have a lot of anger and resentment and bitterness in my heart. Is it too late for me? Please give me some advice and lift me up.

A: When we're struggling for self-confidence, I think we get into trouble when we look at ourselves first. In the business world, if you want something, you've got to go get it. If you want some money, you have to go earn it. If you want some benefit, you have to go after it, go get it, go do it. But that doesn't work with how we relate to our God, does it? The more we depend on ourselves and pressure ourselves to clean ourselves up, the more we see our own sinfulness, our own inner weaknesses. We are then driven even deeper into despair.

When you have feelings such as those described in the question, don't look at yourself. Go to God and look at Him and see what He has done. God has a message for people who struggle, who know they've sinned and who don't like themselves very much, who feel trapped and caught in a prison, a prison of self-doubt, anger, guilt, shame, and resentment toward themselves and others. It's called the Gospel. This is the heart of the message of the Scriptures that help us to break out of those miserable feelings.

The heart of the Gospel is the work of Jesus Christ, our Savior. Speaking in prophecy of the crucifixion of Jesus and His burial and resurrection and what it means, the prophet Isaiah said, **"He was pierced for our transgressions; He was crushed for our iniquities; upon Him was the chastisement that brought us peace, and with His wounds we are healed. All we like sheep have gone astray; we have turned—every one—to his own way"** (53:5–6).

Isaiah says our miseries are our fault. We have contributed our share to the problems and trouble of the world. He includes himself: **"And the LORD has laid on Him the iniquity of *us* all"** (v. 6, emphasis added).

When you are struggling with guilt and self-doubt and depression, you are realizing that you are not worthy of God's blessings. You fear that He might just be punishing you and giving up on you.

The Bible says that *God goes first* in bridging that gap between Him and us. He put His Son on the cross, blamed Him for our sins, and now forgives us. Not sort of halfway in the way that we forgive one another, but *all* the way. *Freely.* No cost, no charge, to you. *Fully.* All your sins have been forgiven. *Unconditionally.* He doesn't make you jump through certain hoops first.

Being saved by the Gospel means that God went first and decided to love you and call a criminal like you lovable. He looks at your ugliness and calls you beautiful. He looks at your prison bonds of fear and guilt and sets you free.

When you realize how much you've been forgiven, that enables you then to do the same thing for the people who have been mean or cruel to you. As you think in your own mind of what God has done to release you of the guilt that you may have, that empowers you to let go of your anger toward other people. The more you think about and enjoy God's Gospel forgiveness of you, the more you can let go of your resentment toward one another. Letting go of your anger not only can restore a broken relationship but also releases you from an anger prison of your own making.

Give that a try. If God thinks you're good looking, then you are good looking. If God thinks you're as holy and pure as His Son, then you really are. If He thinks you're worth something, then you must be. If you are that loved before God, there is power and strength in the Holy Spirit to help you treat the sinful people around you just as kindly.

6

"For the word of the cross is folly to those who are perishing, but to us who are being saved it is the power of God." (1 Corinthians 1:18)

TOUGH TEACHINGS

Q: In a recent message, I felt you incorrectly downplayed people taking antidepressants as a way to cope with life. I have been taking antidepressants, and it took me ten years to find the right medication for my depression. There is depression related to what's going on in a person's life, but then there's clinical depression, which is a medical problem and needs treatment with medication, which I've always viewed as a gift from God, not as a crutch. You wouldn't look at heart medication that way, would you? The way that people in this day and age still view psychological health problems is rather discouraging. No wonder no one wants to talk about them.

A: Thank you for your candor. I owe an apology. In my desire to encourage people to take control of their own emotions and use Scripture's guidance and power, and in my apprehension about the American people's vast appetite for drugs, I overstated a warning about overusing antidepressants. In no way do I ever want to appear to condemn people who are taking medication. I guess I am just overwhelmed by the number of people who are taking antidepressants today, compared to what I remember from my younger days. It seems to me that usage has exploded in our population.

I do agree that clinical depression exists, meaning that the sadness a person feels and the paralysis of self and a negative self-image are not purely based on attitudes that person has chosen, but that there can be a chemical imbalance in a person's brain. I hasten to add, though, that there is also a growing body of literature in medical journals that placebos can sometimes imitate to the same degree the beneficial effects of taking antidepressant medication.

I think we should say in all humility that we don't understand the half of what is going on in the human brain. I think we don't know the half of our own power to control our moods. I advocate for a balanced look at life when we feel the blues.

I don't want to make you feel bad or guilty about yourself when you or your doctor suspect that you are suffering a chemical imbalance and that the appropriate treatment is antidepressants. To be incorporated with that, though, is a great mass of Scripture passages that encourage you and me to know that our mental stability also has a lot to do with the way in which we choose to look at our lives.

There are many, many passages in Scripture that urge us, when we are feeling low, to lift our eyes and look to the Lord. Plenty of Scripture passages urge us to recalibrate our value system. If we're feeling blue because of financial stress or because we don't have a house as big as we want, some of our blues come from materialism. Some of our blues may come from self-pity. Some of our blues come from blaming other people and by refusing to take personal responsibility. You and I can learn to grow out of it and to take control of our own moods.

I think some depressing thoughts and feelings can be relieved by simply admitting our faults, letting God forgive us, and letting go of self-hatred, bad self-images, and habitual thinking. There is healing for the soul and spirit in the message of the Gospel. Our heart can be lifted when we hear God say to us, "I love you"; "You look good to Me"; "I want you in My family forever"; "I'm going to give you gifts;

I have already placed gifts for you in your future; you will find them tomorrow and the day after."

Q: When is it right for us as Christians to judge people?

A: Very tough question. And the reason it's tough is because it seems, at first glance, that the Bible contradicts itself. On the one hand, everybody knows Jesus' famous words from the Sermon on the Mount: **"Judge not, that you be not judged"** (Matthew 7:1). Thus, you can't judge anybody—some people think that means you can't ever say anything critical at all about somebody.

On the other hand, the Lord Jesus also says through His apostle Paul in 1 Corinthians 6:2–3, **"Do you not know that the saints will judge the world? . . . Do you not know that we are to judge angels?"** Paul wrote in Galatians 6:1, **"Brothers, if anyone is caught in any transgression, you who are spiritual should restore him in a spirit of gentleness. Keep watch on yourself, lest you too be tempted."** Clearly, doing some kind of intervention and calling somebody you care about who is involved in some kind of sin—not only are you allowed to do it, but you're even directed to do it.

So which is it? Is judging good or evil? Are we never to say anything critical, or are we commanded to be critical of things that are not right going on in the lives of the people around us? The answer is both. Here, I think, is the difference: When Jesus said, "Do not judge," He wasn't saying, "You may never say anything critical about someone else's sins or problems." What He was saying was, "Don't do God's job. It's not up to you to decree certain penalties for somebody or to imagine that you can read that person's heart." Appropriate: correcting someone's behavior. Inappropriate: passing judgment on the person's worth as a human being or asserting whether you think another Christian's faith is real.

Let's say someone offends you and then says, "I'm sorry," and you say, "You are *not* sorry." We cannot read another person's sincerity. We cannot read what's inside people's hearts. We should keep our comments to people's actions and not speculate on their motives or degree of faith.

Let me give another example. When a husband and wife are having a stressful and tense conversation, sometimes they use words such as, "You always" or "You never." Those are judging words—those words do not deal with a behavior; they deal with the worth of a person. Being helpful as a spiritual friend and counselor is when we say, "What you are doing is wrong." Judging is when we say, "You are evil."

The kind of judging that Jesus condemns involves a hypocritical attitude, where you seem to place yourself above someone else, where you seem to be looking downhill, where you sound patronizing. Nobody wants to hear that kind of stuff. When St. Paul says, **"Keep watch on yourself, lest you too be tempted"** (Galatians 6:1). it's a reminder of how many times you have sinned and perhaps how many times you have benefited from the reclaiming efforts of someone else. When you do your reclaiming efforts and you speak to behaviors, not condemning a person's value and worth, do it humbly, remembering that you're a sinful fool just like that other person. But for the saving mercy of Jesus Christ, we would all perish.

Q: I heard you say once that it's not right to say, "God hates the sin but loves the sinner." What? Do you mean to say that God hates the sinner too?

A: Does God hate sinners or love sinners? The Bible tells us that both of those are true. Now, that seems like a contradiction. But take a look at Exodus 34:5–7 and see how that seeming contradiction is how the Lord God describes Himself. He says—simultaneously—I am a Lord who forgives sin, and I am a Lord who does not leave the guilty unpunished. Well, which is it? Does He forgive sin or punish sin? The answer is both.

Christian theologians call those two messages coming from God "Law and Gospel." Both are true, even though they seem to contradict each other. God simultaneously has wrath for sinners and mercy for sinners. Where this all comes together is on the cross of Christ on Calvary. It was there that God's wrath on sinners was poured out on His Son—and where His mercy on sinners was poured out on us as well.

By grace through faith, you and I receive mercy. Yet we still have a sinner inside of us who needs to tremble appropriately at God's anger. We also need to hear and respect the wrath of God to drive us back over and over to the cross of Christ, where we receive the mercy and forgiveness we need to live.

Q: In the daily news, it seems that there are always reports of natural disasters in the world: flooding in the Midwest, fires in California, earthquakes in China, and the list goes on. If God is in control of nature, why do these things happen to people, even believing people?

A: Jesus' disciples probably had many similar doubts, but as they watched His ministry unfold, they saw clearly the Lord of the universe in action. How they must have been amazed as He manufactured huge amounts of food out of nothing, turned 120 gallons of water into wine, commanded fish to swim into nets, and calmed violent storms. Christ is indeed the Lord of nature.

Someday, believers will witness the re-creation of the universe by the same Lord, who will make a new heaven and a new earth, together at last.

In the meantime, though, nature is sick. St. Paul says in Romans 8 that the creation is in bondage to decay, a curse that God Himself imposed because of human sin. All people on earth must endure physical pain and suffering as part of their curse, but they are also hurt by natural disasters. God promises to limit that destruction for the sake of His children, to make it work for their ultimate good, and to answer prayers with His personal interventions.

The new world that God will create will never again be dangerous to the people who live in it.

Q: What does it mean that all authority is an extension of God's authority? Does that mean I have to obey a government with which I don't agree?

A: Our God is a God of order, not chaos. The plant and animal life that He created on earth reproduces and grows according to amazingly consistent and orderly processes. Even His angels in heaven are ordered in ranks and orders like the military—in fact, the Bible often calls them the heavenly "host" (i.e., army).

God made people to function best when leaders lead and followers follow. This is true of families, churches, neighborhoods, cities, states, and countries. His desire for order is so great that He puts His heavenly authority behind the sinful men and women who wield state power over their citizens. Both Jesus (Matthew 22) and Paul (Romans 13) command obedience and cooperation toward the very governments that would one day order their executions. Cooperation is not an option, even when you don't agree. The exception is when you are commanded to do something that God would call sinful. Peter put it this way: **"We must obey God rather than men"** (Acts 5:29).

Some Christians feel compelled to protest government policies and actions that they are convinced are immoral or are contrary to God's will. There have been times when those protests resulted in arrest and imprisonment. For example, during the civil rights movement in the South, protesters generally bore their civil punishments patiently and bravely, rather than retaliating in revenge, and in this way their moral leadership resulted in important social change in our country. But even those protests showed respect and obedience to the government, since the protesters surrendered peacefully to law officers and accepted the verdicts of the courts that sentenced them.

The Old Testament prophets declared over and over that God watches what kings and armies do with their authority. Since God directs your cooperation and obedience to your government's laws, that means that He takes on Himself the burden of holding governments accountable for how they use their power.

Q: What does it mean that humankind was created in God's image? If humankind was created to be like God, how was it possible for sin to enter the world?

A: The image of God doesn't refer to physical appearance. God is spirit; we are flesh and blood. God's presence fills the universe; we are bound in time and space to one particular place. What that "image" does describe is Adam and Eve's mind-set: they were pure and holy. There was no sin in them. They wanted what God wanted. Their definition of good matched up with God's definition.

Adam and Eve lost God's image by their sin. We regain it through faith in Jesus Christ. God once again regards us as pure and holy in His sight. When we are taken to heaven, we will be glorified and never sin again.

How could two holy people sin? Ah, there's the rub. Believers have been groaning over that dilemma for millennia. There is only one possible answer: God made people to have someone to love, and His great desire is that they love Him back. But love cannot be coerced. It must be freely given. If Adam and Eve were really to have the opportunity to choose to love God, then rejection (with all it implies) had to be possible.

Why would they do it? Why would they trade paradise for hell? You and I get glimmers of that thought process in our own sins. We are God's children now—the Spirit lives in us. However, although we have tasted God's goodness and know in our minds that Satan is evil, we still find His temptations exciting and fulfilling sometimes.

God's last word on this subject will be when we appear before Him, justified and cleansed and holy through the Savior's blood, which we can wear like bridal garments. St. John promises us, **"We know that when [Jesus] appears, we shall be like Him, for we shall see Him as He is. Everyone who has this hope in Him purifies himself, just as He is pure"** (1 John 3:2–3 NIV).

Q: Do you believe in "the rapture"? What is it and what does the Bible say about it?

A: It is a confusing term. In our everyday speech, *rapture* means "bliss." It means "a mental state of great peace and happiness." But the word has another very different meaning, one closer to its etymological source: the Latin verb *rapio,* of which the past participle, *raptus,* gives us *rapture. Rapio* means "to seize and carry away."

In theological circles, the term describes the concept that God will send His holy angels to seize all the believers and carry us up and away from earth.

That concept is beautifully described in 1 Thessalonians 4:13–18. St. Paul tells us that at the end of time, the time of the great judgment, the believers **"will be caught up together with them in the clouds to meet the Lord in the air, and so we will always be with the Lord"** (v. 17). You might call that a "rapture," and I'm all for it.

Unfortunately, it seems that most of the Christians who use the term today mean something different. They have been taught a system of thought that teaches that this rapture is not part of Judgment day, but instead kicks off a thousand-year interim before the judgment. I don't see any of that in 1 Thessalonians 4.

Q: When someone is sick and others are praying for him or her to be healed, if God doesn't heal that person, does it mean that person's faith isn't strong enough or the sickness is somehow that person's fault—maybe because of a sin committed?

A: "Blame the victim" is a nasty trick of the devil's to keep people stuck in their guilt and fear. If you are a believer in Christ, all of your sins, including all the guilt and punishment they may deserve, are put on Christ, and in turn His holiness and favor become ours. Romans 8:1 says that **"there is therefore now no condemnation for those who are in Christ Jesus."** If the sick person is a believer in Christ, then the sickness cannot be thought of as punishment.

Neither should we torture sick people by suggesting that their continuing illness proves that their faith is weak. The power behind any healing is the power of the Lord, not our own power. Even a weak faith in a strong Savior taps into the stream of blessings we receive from Him.

God may send or allow sickness for many reasons:

- to use us as wounded healers for His greater agenda;
- to remind us of our mortality and lift our eyes up to heaven;
- to demonstrate His love and power as He lifts us up later; or
- to toughen us up for the long haul.

Q: I've asked many people to explain the doctrine of predestination but am always left feeling confused. Could you please give me a detailed yet simple explanation that won't leave me still confused?

A: I'll do my best (smile)! First, go directly to God's Word. Don't try to work things out logically from religious ideas you already have in your head. Just let God speak, and a good place to start on this difficult topic is Ephesians 1. Have you read it? It gives us a peek into the vastness of God's mind and purposes, and it stretches the limits of what our brains can process.

Clue 1: God does not tell you about predestination (also called election) so you will completely understand it. It defies neat, tidy human logic. That's okay—God's ways do not have to fit our standards of rightness and justice in order to be true and good.

Clue 2: Neither does this teaching help you look around and determine "who's in and who's out." That's God's job—let Him do it His way, on His terms, and on His schedule.

Clue 3: He tells you about His eternal choosing for one main purpose alone: *so that you give all glory and praise for your salvation to Him.* Everything you do your believing and your good works—

are simply responses to His saving grace to you, not the basis for His decision to love you and call you His child.

Q: What are people talking about when they speak of the age of accountability for children? Does this mean that children aren't responsible for their sin and will go to heaven if they die young?

A: The "age of accountability" is a well-meaning but false concept. The Bible does not teach any such thing. It is a comfort, I guess, to suppose that children twelve or younger (the usual age put forth) do not bear any responsibility for their sins of being and doing, but the Bible does not offer that comfort. This concept is man-made. What the Bible does say is that damnable sin begins at birth, or more accurately, from the time of conception (see Psalm 51:5). Dying young has no biblical guarantee for automatic entrance into paradise. Children need the Savior as much as grown-ups do (**"Let the little children come to Me"** Matthew 19:14).

Q: I recently had a miscarriage. I have so many questions to which I can't seem to find answers. Is my baby in heaven? How will I know him or her when God takes me there?

A: My heart hurts for your loss and for all women who have suffered miscarriages. God's Word tells us only part of what we would like to know; we'll have to wait to "know as we are known," in St. Paul's words (see 1 Corinthians 13:12).

The Word reveals in Psalm 139:13 that God Himself lavishes divine care in designing every life in the womb: **"You formed my**

inward parts; You knitted me together." The unborn John the Baptist leaped for joy in His mother's womb—a miracle, to be sure, but also an indication that the jumper was a person, filled with the Holy Spirit (Luke 1:44).

The Bible tells us that saving faith is created and sustained in people through Word and Sacraments. But it doesn't give a clear teaching on the eternal destiny of unborn babies who are miscarried, aborted, or stillborn—little ones whom we had no chance to baptize and teach. We should content ourselves with what God has clearly said and hold off putting out personal opinions, even pious opinions, as divine truth.

We know that God is absolutely just and totally loving. We know that He created this life in the womb, and each unborn baby that didn't make it to a healthy birth has a distinct DNA. The God who didn't flinch from offering up His only Son on the cross can be trusted to handle this problem in the perfect way. We'll find out soon.

Our loved ones in heaven will be raised up fully healthy and restored, not in the condition in which their bodies perished. God has the blueprints on file. We will be our ideal selves—it will be a joy to rediscover our loved ones and friends. God will help you find them all.

Q: In a recent message, you used a term I've not heard used before: *pre-forgiveness*. You remember the first word Jesus used at the beginning of His first sermon, which is *repent*. Just before His ascension, He said, "Repentance and forgiveness of sins will be preached . . . to all nations" (Luke 24:27 NIV) Where does repentance fit with this concept of pre-forgiveness?

A: When I made up the word *pre-forgiveness,* what I was trying to convey was the scriptural idea that the price of your salvation was already paid before you were born. Your forgiveness was purchased before you even existed, obviously before you had ever committed any sins yourself. That's where the salvation story begins. Objectively, universally, and with love, Jesus Christ—who lived long before you—paid your price, made you His own, and declared His love for you. *In advance:* that's what I mean by pre-forgiveness. You already had a "not guilty" verdict pronounced on you before you sinned even once.

Now, that does not mean that repentance and faith are irrelevant. Wrong! The Bible says we are saved by grace *through faith.* The mighty Gospel message gives you the ability to want to repent of your sins and turn in faith to the Lord Jesus.

Q: I was watching a recent telecast of *Time of Grace,* and I heard you say that God does not like us to ask for signs. If that's the case, why did He not only allow people like Gideon to ask for signs but He also sent the signs? I'm confused by this, and it makes God seem purely arbitrary.

A: The biblical record is abundantly clear that God often sent or used supernatural signs to back up the message of the prophets and apostles. What God does not like is when people ignore His clear Word and instead just want to see signs. St. Paul (1 Corinthians 1:20–21) and Jesus (Matthew 12:39) spoke very harshly about sign seeking that ignores God's clear words. Jesus told Satan himself not to put the Lord God to the test (Luke 4:12), that is, set up a man-made "proving" experiment.

Gideon indeed asked for a special sign, two actually, and God chose to grant his requests. I'd go easy on using Gideon as a role model, however. God bore with some very weak behaviors on the part of His patriarchs and judges. He was patient with them, especially when they were faced with extreme situations, and He used them in spite of their weaknesses. His direct appearance and promises should have been enough for Gideon. But God in mercy gave him what he asked for.

I might mention also that Satan masquerades as an angel of light (2 Corinthians 11:14). You don't want to fall for any of his tricks or stunts disguised as signs. The safest beacon for knowing the right path is God's wonderful Word.

Q: Why does God let my mother experience so much pain in her old age? What can I say to help her?

A: Your mom's situation is not unusual. Everybody has pain and everybody suffers. Everybody has a load to haul. However, some people's loads just seem so much heavier than those of others. There is no rational explanation for why bad things happen—they are random. Why does one of my loved ones have leukemia? Why has another had not one but two marriages break up? Why was another born with Williams syndrome, leaving him with some lifelong physical struggles?

We all groan and wait for heaven. God sees that the earth and all its people are broken, and He gives us treats and repairs and boosts to keep us going. But this world is going to be destroyed. So if your mom realizes that there is nothing for her here, that's a good thing. We look forward to a world without pain, sorrow, or suffering. The sweet thing is that Jesus' gift is free to all. It is not for those who have deserved it, but given freely to all who want it.

Just tell your mom the truth—that Jesus loves her, that He hurts when she hurts, and that He will come soon for her. In the meantime, we want to let God use us and use our situations to be helpful to Him in any way. Read John 9 about the man born blind. His disability was not a punishment for evil. His disability became a platform so **"that the works of God might be displayed in him"** (v. 3).

7

"In My Father's house are many rooms. If it were not so, would I have told you that I go to prepare a place for you?" (John 14:2)

DEATH AND HEAVEN

Q: At the time of death, do our souls immediately go to heaven? I was with my mother when she died. I asked her if she could see Jesus and she said, "Yes." A woman in our congregation said she couldn't have and that she was in some form of death, meaning that she must have been totally unconscious, not able to be aware of anything. I don't understand when, where, or what happens in the resurrection of believers.

A: I think every believer has wondered about those things at one time or another. The Lord truly has not yet revealed the full story of the things that will happen after we die, and He gives only a number of small statements and clues.

Here, though, is what God does say: Your body literally dies, and it goes back to the earth from which it was made, ashes to ashes and dust to dust. Your physical body does go back to being part of the earth. But God will have absolutely no trouble putting it back together. In fact, 1 Corinthians 15:52 says that He will reassemble you **"in a moment, in the twinkling of an eye, at the last trumpet"** (in other words, on Judgment Day).

Even while you are waiting for that mighty trumpet sound, your soul, or spirit, does live on. There are a number of fascinating examples in Scripture to show that consciousness does continue and that in your soul, or spirit, you in effect have a private judgment day and either go to hell or go to heaven *in spirit.* For the hell component, just think of what happened to the Lord Jesus Himself. We read in 1 Peter 3 says that after Jesus rose from the dead, the very first thing He did, even before walking out of the tomb on Easter Sunday morning, was to go in spirit to the nether regions of hell and proclaim His great triumph to the souls and spirits of the disobedient who now live there permanently.

Remember also that right before He died, Jesus said to a repentant criminal who was dying next to Him, **"Today you will be with Me in Paradise"** (Luke 23:43). The simplest meaning of those words is that *"today* you will see Me and My Father and the Holy Spirit and the souls of the saints and the beloved of God in heaven." *Today.* Although on the original "today" the criminal's body would be thrown in a ditch or buried somewhere, *today* he would see God. That could only be true because by Jesus' words from the cross next to him he was already with the Lord.

Revelation 6:9–10 states, **"I saw under the altar the souls of those who had been slain for the word of God and for the witness they had borne. They cried out with a loud voice, 'O Sovereign Lord, holy and true, how long before You will judge and avenge our blood on those who dwell on the earth?'"** This passage clearly shows that there is awareness, there is consciousness and the ability to communicate with God already in heaven *before* Judgment Day.

Do the souls of believers enter into the presence of the Lord immediately when they die? I think the answer that Scripture presents to us is yes. Is it possible that some believers have already gotten their first glimpses of heavenly glory before they are fully dead? In my opinion, yes.

Q: I have a question about cremation. My congregation has never accepted that way for final rites. Last spring, a member of our church who passed away was cremated. I have discussed this with my friends and years ago researched my concordance and Bible for anything about it. Nowhere in the Bible is it discussed. There is a cemetery next to my property, and I heard the grave diggers talking: some of them are unbelievers, and even *they* don't think it's right. So I'm opposed to it. Do we have to follow what heathens have done and are doing? I think not.

A: Ahem . . . that's not a question; it's a statement (smile). I think this questioner has pretty much made up his mind. If in your own mind, you think cremation is wrong and you want to make sure that the loved ones whose funerals you organize involve the traditional method of a casket, a viewing, the vault, and all of the rituals that have long been associated with funerals, then that's how you ought to do it. Cremation in my grandfather's time carried more of a stigma among Christians because it seemed to carry with it an attitude of atheistic defiance: "Let's see God try to put *this* body together again!" But I don't hear that view anymore today.

There's a clue in what this writer says, and that's that you can page through your entire Bible from front to back and you won't see any words of God that either encourage or condemn the practice of cremation.

When the Bible neither commands nor forbids a practice, it is called an *adiaphoron*. That's a Greek word that describes a "middle zone" in which God has placed the decision in the realm of your personal judgment. If you think that cremation is disrespectful of the dead or displeasing to God, then don't do it.

Another example of an adiaphoron is a dress code in church. There's nothing in the Bible that gives specific directions as to how people ought to dress when they go to church. When people ask me how they should dress in church, I say, "In a way that communicates from you to your God how much you love being in His house." If you can serve God best by being casual, then dress casually and be there with a smile. If you show extra respect for God by putting on a jacket or even putting on a tie, then do that. Or if you're a female and you don't want to wear slacks, if you just feel more respectful and worshipful in a dress in God's house, then wear a dress.

On the one hand, it is not a sin to wear slacks to church; nor is it a sin if you choose to do the process called cremation. If you are organizing the funeral of someone you love, if you are the executor of that estate, or if you open a will and the deceased leaves instructions, "I wish to be cremated," and you have to carry out those instructions, you are not sinning.

Frankly, I see value in both practices. Having a traditional funeral offers some significant advantages. There can be a viewing, which can provide closure for people who perhaps did not have a chance to be there in the person's last days. It may help people feel a personal connection one last time. I have heard that it might be especially good for children if they can see the deceased—that way, it's brought home to them that the person is really dead.

On the other hand, I see value in cremation. A traditional full funeral can be expensive; cremation is significantly cheaper. It may be that in his or her estate plans, someone would prefer that assets go to benefit some people or a ministry rather than being spent on embalming, casket, vault, and full-sized cemetery plot. Another advantage if the body isn't being embalmed for viewing is that there is no time pressure and you have more flexibility for scheduling the memorial service. But in all things, when we use the words *right* and *wrong, evil,* or *sinful* and *good*, let's limit ourselves to those things that God has clearly identified that way in His Word.

Q: If a ninety-two-year-old man in declining health makes a wish to die, is that a sin against God?

A: Depends. If he has come to hate his life, has grown deaf to the Word of God, and is knowingly planning suicide, he is sinning indeed. I used to visit an older man named Fred who made sure I knew about the gun on his coffee table. I warned him as gently but firmly as I could about his suicide talk. Imagine my shock and dismay when his son called me to tell me that Fred had used it on himself. We always need to take suicide talk very seriously. The evil one works day and night to break our spirit and tempt us to despair.

On the other hand, wishing that God would speed up His timetable and come to take you home is a sweet thought. St. Paul himself said, **"To die is gain. . . . My desire is to depart and be with Christ, for that is far better"** (Philippians 1:21–23). Those are not thoughts of despair, self-hatred, or rebellion, but the confident utterance of a person who knows he's loved and forgiven and is certain of his eternal destiny. It is also the statement of a man who didn't hasten his eternity with suicide but was content to let the Lord measure the length of his life. In the meantime, as he longingly waited, he knew that he had work to do: **"If I am to live in the flesh, that means fruitful labor for me"** (Philippians 1:22).

Q: Who will be in heaven?

A: Finally—an easy question. God has answered this one in the clearest possible way. May I quote the passage on so many stadium signs? **"God so loved the world, that He gave His only Son,**

that *whoever believes in Him* **should not perish but have eternal life"** (John 3:16, emphasis added). Of course, our triune God—Father, Son, and Holy Spirit—will be there as well, along with ten thousand times ten thousand holy angels in all their ranks and orders.

Q: Are there different levels in heaven (based on the many mansions), where the levels depend upon how strong your faith was and how much you did for the Lord while on earth?

A: What awaits people after the great judgment is more complex than it seems. On the one hand, the Bible often describes a simple division—the believers and unbelievers, the sheep and the goats (Matthew 25), the saved and the condemned, those going to heaven and those going to hell.

On the other hand, Scripture also describes many levels of punishment. Mark 12:40a; Matthew 11:24; and Luke 12:47 all demonstrate that the more you know, the greater your accountability. Some "will be beaten with many blows," some with few (Luke 12:47 NIV).

Scripture also gives little glimpses and hints that heaven's rewards and new roles will not be one-size-fits-all. Luke 18–19 suggest varying degrees of reward for believers. Daniel 12:2–3 says, **"Many of those who sleep in the dust of the earth shall awake, some to everlasting life, and some to shame and everlasting contempt. And those who are wise shall shine like the brightness of the sky above; and those who turn many to righteousness, like the stars forever and ever."**

God lets us peek at these things not to stimulate our competitive instincts and to jockey for position. Jesus had a severe scolding for His disciples James and John when they wanted positions of power in the new age to come. I think God shows us little rays of glory to get us excited and to assure us that our exertions and sacrifices and suffering this side of the grave are noted and remembered. St. Paul said, **"At that time each will receive his praise from God"** (1 Corinthians 4:5 NIV).

Q: My friend's young son died recently in an accident. I just can't understand it—he was only four. How could God let a tragedy like this happen to a Christian family?

A: We may learn the *why* or we may never know this side of heaven. We live in a broken world: people are sick, and even nature itself is in bondage to corruption (Romans 8:21). The apostle James reminds us, **"What is your life? For you are a mist that appears for a little time and then vanishes"** (James 4:14). No one is guaranteed nine pleasant decades and then a sweet, painless slide into the grave. We are all living out the original divine curse on Adam and Eve's rebellion, **"You are dust, and to dust you shall return"** (Genesis 3:19).

It may have been a huge blessing, you know. God may have seen that that little boy was at his absolute peak of faith at age 4 and that if he would have lived to be forty he would have lost his faith and reverted to being an unbeliever. Maybe God took him at four to make sure he would spend eternity with his Christian family. What we can be sure of is this: if God let it happen, then He's okay with it, and we can be too. It means He has a plan to bring blessing out of the pain. He will continue to work all things for good for those who love Him.

Young people die. Children die. Babies die. Everybody needs to be connected with Jesus Christ, and the earlier the better. The Word and Baptism are for everybody—don't wait with either. Jesus said, **"Let the children come to Me, and do not hinder them, for to such belongs the kingdom of God"** (Luke 18:16). Every Christian child who dies in the Lord will rise again in the Lord just as surely as Jairus's sixth-grade daughter did (Luke 8).

Q: If the devil was an angel in heaven, how could he have sinned? Will it be possible for sin to enter heaven when I'm there after I die?

A: Satan was indeed an angel in heaven. The prophet Ezekiel, speaking first to the evil king of Tyre and then to the prince of darkness, said that Satan had originally been ordained one of the guardian cherubim, walking amidst the fire stones of heaven. But **"your heart was proud because of your beauty; you corrupted your wisdom for the sake of your splendor"** (Ezekiel 28:17). The power to offer true love and obedience to God always comes with the terrible power to offer rebellion and disobedience.

Satan will not have access to the believers in heaven. You will be safe, for he will be thrown into the lake of burning sulfur, there to be tormented day and night for ever and ever (Revelation 20:10). You will never be tempted again; nor will you ever sin again.

Q: Why did Jesus have to rise from the dead?

A: The Bible says that **"[Jesus] was delivered up for our trespasses and raised for our justification"** (Romans 4:25). Jesus Himself explained to the two Emmaus disciples on Easter Sunday afternoon, **"Was it not necessary that the Christ should suffer these things and enter into His glory?"** (Luke 24:26). In the Father's grand design, the resurrection proved that death could not hold onto Christ. His resurrection guarantees our forgiveness. His resurrection also guarantees our resurrection.

Q: Recently, a friend of my son's hanged himself. My son is very upset about this. My son had fallen away from the Church, but since this tragedy he is asking me many questions. How does the Church deal with those who feel messed up throughout life, taking drugs and alcohol for comfort and then leaving a note and taking their lives? I feel God has opened a door for me to reach out to my son, and I want to make sure I act and respond correctly and with compassion.

A: I am sorry to hear about the tragedy that has come into your family and the family of your son's friend. When a person commits suicide, it raises many questions; questions that are not always easy to answer. In times such as these, we look to God's Word for help and guidance.

Taking one's life is obviously not God's will. It is self-murder and it is sin. If the young man was not a Christian, then we need to be honest with what God says and understand that the young man will not be heaven, for **"whoever does not believe will be condemned"** (Mark 16:16). His death then becomes a sad reminder for us as to what happens to those living outside of the kingdom of God. Unfortunately, we don't know with certainty what is in a person's heart. When someone dies who was exhibiting an attitude of contempt for God, we fear the worst.

Nevertheless, the act of suicide, like any sin, isn't the final deciding factor for where a person spends eternity. The core issue is the person's relationship with Jesus Christ. If the young man still had a Christian faith—even though troubled, confused, and living a messed-up life—we can find comfort in knowing that those who trust in Christ will be saved. Jesus Christ died to bring forgiveness for *all* sins. Was this young man who committed suicide a believer in Jesus who acted rashly in a momentary weakness of faith? I have personally presided over the funerals of people who took their own lives, but I had seen enough evidence of their faith to assume that they were suffering from terrible depression and mental illness, not a complete loss of faith.

When there is any doubt at all about a person's faith in Christ, let us give the benefit of the doubt and give the whole business to God to sort out. In the meantime, the sad occasion gives us an abundance of opportunities to bring the saving message of Jesus to people left behind who are hurting and sad.

Q: Will we become angels when we die?

A: There's a great amount of confusion in people's minds about the next life. A certain pseudo-Christian mythology has arisen from popular talk, television, and magazines that repeats and perpetuates popular myths and misconceptions. None of it is from the Bible. We will not become angels. The angels were designed to be angels and will stay angels. We were designed to be people and will stay people. The angels are our servants. They are our protectors, providers, and sometimes heralds and messengers. **"Are [angels] not all ministering spirits sent out to serve for the sake of those who are to inherit salvation?"** (Hebrews 1:14). You will have a physical body. They won't.

Q: Will we have physical bodies or be spirit beings?

A: We will be spirit beings first, between the time of our death and the Day of Judgment. When the archangel Michael blows his trumpet, the bodies of all the dead will arise, and you and I will get our material bodies back. We will not be turned into virtual humans. We'll still be ourselves—flesh and blood, real people. You will look like you, only without the flaws. No more limping, no more badly set broken bones, no more glasses, no more fillings in your teeth, no more prosthetic limbs. I suppose if bald guys really have gotten to like their baldness, they could ask to keep it. But I'm expecting that an awful lot of guys with hair loss will ask for their hair back.

Q: Will there be marriage in heaven?

A: Jesus did say we would be like angels in one respect: we will neither marry nor be given in marriage (Luke 20:35). This is both a thrilling and, perhaps to some, disappointing feature of life in heaven. God will have a new relationship design for us. I think it will be like one big family reunion. We'll be in love with everybody. Nobody will ever again be a threat to you. You'll never have to lock the doors of your house again. Nobody's going to rip you off. Everybody you meet will be your friend. I think that feeling of being surrounded by human love, in addition to being surrounded by God's love, will be a more-than-adequate replacement for the exclusive love that husbands and wives enjoy now. I think I'm pretty safe in assuring you that you will not be disappointed by any aspect of God's new design for your heavenly life.

Q: What about our loved ones who aren't in heaven? Won't we be sad for them?

A: We will experience utter serenity when we are with the Lord. Isaiah 65:17 says, **"The former things shall not be remembered or come into mind."** The painful memories of the past will be gone. Either God will selectively erase our memories and it just won't occur to us, or He'll allow us to remember but make the memories cause us no pain. Either way, the painful things won't come to mind; all tears will be wiped from our eyes. All the saints will concur with the Lord's decisions. Revelation 19:1–2 says, **"I heard what seemed to be the loud voice of a great multitude in heaven, crying out, 'Hallelujah! Salvation and glory and power belong to our God, for His judgments are true and just.'"** That is to say, if you become aware that somebody you loved on earth is not numbered among the believers, you will understand the rightness of all of God's decisions of judgment.

Q: I love to eat. Heaven to me will include food. What do you think?

A: I've read all kinds of amazing statements from otherwise clear-minded, sober commentators who somehow assume that we're not really going to eat physical food anymore. That is just mind-boggling to me. Is there something inherently gross or evil or disgusting about food or the human body? Did not Jesus Christ in His resurrected body enjoy a breakfast of fish with His disciples (John 21)? Was that food not digested in His divine, resurrected body? Will we not be raised in our actual bodies? Will we then be powered by heavenly ethanol or angelic batteries instead of metabolizing starch and protein?

The Bible often refers to the experience of heaven as a great feast (see Matthew 22, for example). I find it hard to think that those are only metaphors. Jesus promised His disciples on Maundy Thursday evening that the next time they would drink wine together would be in His Father's kingdom (Matthew 26:29).

God may surprise us with something different, but until further notice, I am planning to eat food in our new physical world.

Q: Will we sit on clouds and sing eternal praises?

A: You've read too many cartoons about clouds and harps. Heaven isn't going to be eight million bazillion years of cloud-sitting or unending choir practice. Jesus said once, **"My Father is working until now, and I am working"** (John 5:17). May I dare to suggest that we, too, will work in God's presence? I think we will have jobs. On your best days, you kind of like work, don't you? Wouldn't it be wonderful if every day were like that?

In the parable of the ten minas (Luke 19), Jesus implies that after the judgment the King will have further and greater responsibilities for those who did His will.

I would imagine that that's what God is designing for you. I can imagine jobs of service, in which we will joyfully do things for one another. Those of you who are good organizers of people and events will keep doing that, and you will love your work. God will give you work that clicks with your ability and passion. I can imagine that Johann Sebastian Bach will be writing music again, telling of the great works of God. Great literature will continue to be produced. We will need storytellers and musicians and painters, builders and craftsmen, weavers and cooks.

Q: Please explain why you think Jesus has His human form in heaven.

A: After His triumphant descent into hell *in spirit,* Jesus had a *bodily* resurrection. **"Touch Me, and see. For a spirit does not have flesh and bones as you see that I have"** (Luke 24:39). He ate broiled fish with His disciples. Jesus then took His body with Him to heaven. That's taught in the accounts of the ascension, both at the end of the Gospel of Luke and also in the first chapter of Acts.

How can this be? Where did He go? Is there an oxygen-rich atmosphere in an actual spatial location where Jesus is now? We don't know. But we do know this: **"When He appears we shall be like Him, because we shall see Him as He is"** (1 John 3:2). Just as He is resurrected to new life *with His body,* we will be resurrected with our bodies too. Cleansed, purified, strengthened, and freed from all disabilities of age and illness, we will be 100 percent again!

Q: I can't imagine heaven being heaven without being able to hold my wife's hand, hug her, and spend eternity with her and the Lord. I know that Scripture says there won't be marrying or giving in marriage in heaven, but do you believe we'll continue those special relationships with our Christian spouses in heaven?

A: Here's what we know: We will **"neither marry nor [be] given in marriage"** (Luke 20:35). We will live with resurrected bodies and still be ourselves. We will still have our names and personalities. We will know one another. We will work to serve the Lord and one another. It's probably a good thing that earthly marriages aren't eternal, or else widows who remarry on earth would have an awkward three-way marriage in heaven.

Here's a thought: Just because we are not going to be bonded permanently to another human being any longer doesn't mean that we can't have special relationships or even live together. I would guess that the lips in our resurrected bodies will prove useful not only for speaking and eating food but might also prove handy for kissing. I also doubt that hugging will be a forbidden activity. If you really loved someone on earth, why would that love necessarily stop in heaven?

Q: Why doesn't God tell us more about heaven in the Bible?

A: The Bible is silent on a great many topics, and one of those is a detailed description of specifically what our lives will be like in heaven. I think God probably has very good reasons for providing only hints. I suspect He thinks that we can't handle the fullness of it all because we might obsess over the material aspects and misunderstand the freedoms and new ways of living. God is like a father or mother who has assembled a great many presents but makes His eager children wait until Christmas Eve to open them. Just as parents will tease their children with clues and hints, God does tell us enough to thrill our hearts at the beauty and peace of it all. **"Now we see in a mirror dimly, but then face to face. Now I know in part; then I shall know fully"** (1 Corinthians 13:12).

Old Testament

New Testament

Topical Index